from BOOMERS *to* BLOGGERS

SUCCESS STRATEGIES ACROSS GENERATIONS

BY **MISTI BURMEISTER**
CEO, INSPIRION, INC.

synergy press

FROM BOOMERS TO BLOGGERS,
Copyright © 2008 by Misti Burmeister. All rights reserved.
Printed in the United States of America. No part of this book
may be used or reproduced in any manner whatsoever without written
permission except in the case of brief quotations embodied in
critical articles and reviews. For information, address
Synergy Press, LLC, 11489 Carriage Gate Court, Fairfax, VA 22030.

Synergy Press books may be purchased in bulk for educational, business,
or sales promotional use. For information please write:
Special Markets Department, Synergy Press, LLC
11489 Carriage Gate Court, Fairfax, VA 22030

telephone: 703.865.6033
email: order@synergypressonline.com

FIRST EDITION

Designed by Jennifer Tyson

Library of Congress Cataloging-in-Publishing Data

Burmeister, Misti L., 1978-
From Boomers To Bloggers: Success Strategies Across
Generations / Misti Burmeister. — 1st ed.
     p. cm.
     Includes references.
     ISBN: 978-0-9802209-0-2
     1. Leadership
     2. Employee Retention-United States.
     3. Organizational change.
     4. Generations-United States
     I. Title

DEDICATION

I am dedicating this book to my partner, Yvette Nash.
Thank you for believing in me, supporting me,
and helping me refocus a billion times. Your calm
spirit and tough love have helped make this
(and many others) project a huge success.

thank you!

ACKNOWLEDGEMENTS

There is absolutely NO way I could have written this book without the help of SO many incredible people. These individuals have been enormously generous with their time, energy and resources. Without them, none of this would have been possible. In order to conserve space (and trees!), I'll forgo the amazing stories associated with each person's participation.

I WOULD LIKE TO THANK THE FOLLOWING PEOPLE FOR THEIR CONTRIBUTION TO MY LIFE AND TO THIS BOOK:

Jim and Eileen Burmeister, Yvette Nash, Faye Levow, Jennifer Tyson, Xavier Williams, Jeffery Tobias Halter, Vannessa Moran, Robert White, Carolyn Martin, Ken Kaufman, Pam Krulitz, Edie Frazer, Randy Schools, Tony Wolfe, Lori Addicks, Steve Dorfman, Masoud Edalatkhah, Mali Phonpadith, Carolyn Franke, Sue Snyder, Marie Dudek, Jacob Steele, Sally Strackbein, Eric Habermann, Cam and Penny Boyce, Steve Haddad, Bea Fields, Laila Wardak, Sandra King, Stephanie McFee, Andres Fossas, Gary Gadson, Sherilyn Marrow, Jim Keaton, Alex Couloumbis, Debra Slover, Rob Silva, Stephanie Miller, Sue Wiman, Raine and Jeff Hickman, Paul Barnett, Brian Paris, DJ Frazier, Tony Mazraani, Lin Allen, Ann-Marie Triolo, Hope Brill, Cary Kemp, Robert Fleischmann, Steven Hady, Ken Barrett, Jim Harrison, Myralyn Supetran, Leah Rampy, Sarah Galbraith, Jennifer Deal, Corey Blake, Kevin LaMontagne, Melissa Pope, David Palmer, Doug Francis, Rita Seelig Ayers, Lee Self, Jonathan and Carrie Kraft, Jean Palmer, W. Stanton Smith, Eric Marterella, Paul Mcrae, Ben Casnocha, Laura Miles-Bailey, Cathy Sparks, David Cohen, Beth Halbert, Mike Masterson, Sherry Lowry, Michael Reuter, Darren Livingston, Charlotte Pandraud, Samuel Betances, Alan Croll, Adrienne Onder, Brian Macleod, Jack Garson, Cathy Backinger, Bill Howe, Carol Adrienne, Zig Ziglar, Dick and Diane Gottron, Mary Jo Shevlin, Kim Dixon, Doug Patterson, Svetlana Kim, Ellen Shadur, Frank Hoffman, Freddi Donner, Fred Farmer, Paul Girardi, Gail Johnson, Kishau Rogers, Janet Wigfield, Jan Beauregard, Pilar Jimenez, Jill Ellefson, Jason Lalak, Kathryn Mahoney, Karina Wilhelms, Kerri and Jim Rocco, Linda Wind, Linda Maslar, Lorna Donatone, Mary Schnack, Nelson Frye, Philip Martin, Phyllis Endicott, Antonella and Eric Nash, Pat Stipe, Zenia Sahadeo, Skip Yowell, Toni Little, Teresa Persons, Jean Kramlich, Jimmy Burmeister, Billy Coleman, Dick and Dian Gottron, Art Dwight, Matt Hamilton.

I appreciate you for putting up with me, pushing me to think deeper, guiding me, supporting me, helping me stay true to my vision, and ensuring I kept faith in myself. Your kindness will continue to ripple throughout the world. Thank you!

CONTENTS

from BOOMERS *to* BLOGGERS

SUCCESS STRATEGIES ACROSS GENERATIONS

FOREWORD

AS A MEMBER OF THE ORIGINAL ME GENERATION, I JUMPED AT THE OPPORTUNITY TO CONTRIBUTE TO THIS BOOK BY A GEN YER. ANYTHING WE BABY BOOMERS CAN DO TO SUPPORT YOUNG PROFESSIONALS WHO PAY INTO SOCIAL SECURITY IS A WISE BUSINESS DECISION.

I first met Misti Burmeister through our mutual participation in the Gen Y Project. I'm Chapter 4 and she's Chapter 19 in *Millennial Leaders: Success Stories from Today's Most Brilliant Generation Y Leaders* (Bea Fields, Scott Wilder, Jim Bunch and Rob Newbold [NY: Morgan James, 2008]).

What impressed me most about Misti's work is the balanced approach she takes to a topic that has caused consternation at best, and conflict at worst, for the past 15 years: generational diversity in the workplace. When did age become such a contentious workplace issue?

Travel back with me to the early 1990s when older generations, who grew up with the age-respecting system called seniority, first encountered visitors from another planet: those young, arrogant, disloyal slackers dubbed Generation X.

"I'll be loyal to your organization," Gen Xers said, "*until* I get a better deal. Hopefully, it's with you, in some part of your organization. But if not, don't take it personally. I'm responsible for my life and my career."

Xers weren't trying to be difficult, they were merely responding to a world that had changed; a world driven by fierce competition, globalization, technology, broken promises, and the demise of job security.

By the late 90s, some organizations earned the just-in-time loyalty of this talented group by offering flexible schedules, a variety of career paths, increasing spheres of responsibility, coaching-style managers and mentors — all Gen X motivators.

Others, to this day, are still grappling with the Gen X challenge, while finding themselves overwhelmed by the next wave of upstarts. If they thought Gen Xers were problematic, they are flummoxed by their younger siblings: the upbeat, optimistic, super techno-savvy, entrepreneurial, entitled, life-long learners, variously called the Millennials, Echo-Boomers, Creative Connecteds, and, most commonly, Generation Y.

Suddenly, Baby Boomers are stymied by the fact that they are now managing, or being managed by, people young enough to be their children.

While members of the Me Generation admit they incubated their Mini-Me's with an "I can do anything I want." attitude and "I'm entitled to the opportunity to do it," they have a hard time coping with these expectations at work.

Likewise, Gen Xers, forgetting about the curves they threw their managers not long ago, are exasperated with Gen Yers. "They want feedback, recognition, and new experiences every fifteen minutes!" one complains.

"I don't understand how they can juggle nine instant messages, but can't focus on one task," another adds.

And the beat goes on.

Enter Misti Burmeister, a Gen Y researcher, trainer, and coach, who has racked up some hard-earned wisdom based on hard-knock experience.

Several years ago, she recognized the disconnect among generations and their inability to focus on what unites, rather than divides them: the mission and vision of an organization; the need to create a career plan for those just starting or redefining their jobs; and the importance of seizing every opportunity to gain and share experience.

Rather than embrace "blameology," Misti puts responsibility for multi-generational communication squarely where it needs to be: on the shoulders of each person of each generation. She advises young professionals to "Do what needs to be done without complaining, be patient, consistently communicate your career aspirations with the right people and do what's necessary for the success of the company."

She reminds seasoned pros that "The long-term success of your organization depends on the success of young professionals. Take the time to mentor and coach them ... They need your help in seeing the big picture, creating a career plan and gaining the necessary experience to set them up for success."

Misti's message is refreshing, her advice practical. Throw in a sense of urgency and it becomes even more valuable. Boomers are beginning to retire in record numbers (some experts predict that, by 2011, 11,500 will retire every day) and Xers and Yers are already the majority of the workforce (52% as of this writing). Literally, the changing-of-the-guard is happening right now, and, no matter what our age, we need each other.

Young pros need to gain experience quickly and clarify the values that will guide their careers. Seasoned pros can help them do that.

Baby Boomers need to ensure a lasting legacy — and, perhaps, secure their pensions and Social Security — by developing the next generations of leaders to propel their organizations well into the 21st century.

Thank you, Misti, for tackling this topic head-on and inspiring everyone in every generation to take responsibility for their lives, their careers, and the success of their organizations.

CAROLYN A. MARTIN, PH.D.
Principal
RainmakerThinking, Inc.
www.rainmakerthinking.com

Co-author of **Managing the Generation Mix:**
From Urgency to Opportunity.
Second Expanded Edition.
(Amherst, MA: HRD Press, 2006)

INTRODUCTION

As a seasoned professional, have you ever wondered how to best tap into and utilize the talents and skills of the youngest generation? Have you wondered how to get them to care about their work, show up on time and do what needs to get done without complaining about flex-time, holidays or promotions?

What if you learned everything you needed to know to effectively motivate, inspire and create results within every generation?

What if every employee *wanted* to be led by you?

What if every company and leader wanted *you* on their team?

What if you were more employable, rather than merely employed?

Have you wondered how companies like Google and Disney have created an environment to retain their talent? How about award-winning companies like Post Properties? Post is a national property management company that has created an award-winning internship program which sources a talent pool of dedicated employees for their future. This book will give you insight into how these winning corporations have kept their most valuable resources — their people, and how their people find fulfillment in their work.

In his book *Decoding Generational Differences: Fact, fiction ... or should we just get back to work?* W. Stanton Smith shares this critical information: "Gen X presents a much smaller pool of available workers, and will not be able to fill the positions left vacant by retirements. By 2008, the pool of available workers among 25-44 year olds will have decreased by 7% from the level five years previous (2003), resulting in a significant labor shortage. In fact, every year for the next 30 years, there will be fewer young people to replace retiring workers. The labor shortages will continue well into the future, as average annual growth of the workforce is projected to hover at around 1% through 2015."

So, as seasoned professionals are beginning their move into retirement, organizations are required to find ways to attract, retain and motivate *across generations.* This book explores the best methods for organizations and individuals to attain their respective goals.

While there have been many books written to help seasoned professionals and organizations better attract, retain and motivate the youngest generation, I have not yet seen a book that assists both young and seasoned professionals effectively communicate with each other. There has also been a fair amount of finger pointing, suggesting that one or the other generation must conform to the other's desires. I believe, teach and have experienced how mutual understanding, communication and a focus on an organization's vision and mission provide professionals of all generations a satisfying work experience with strong growth opportunities.

Let me share with you why I feel this topic of generational communication is *so* important.

A young woman stood up in my audience at a prominent coaching and leadership development conference and asked, "What is my responsibility in bridging this communication gap? How can I help?"

She, like many in her generation, wants nothing more than to find the right words, learn the right tricks and gain the right visibility to advance her career, while helping her organization reach its goals. Many simply don't have the "right" words and actions to demonstrate this desire to seasoned professionals.

She believes, as I do, that she could do something to bridge this generational gap. While most books and generational speakers address how organizations and seasoned professionals need to "deal with" the younger generation, I believe something entirely different. I believe the only way to bridge the generational gap is to address how both seasoned **and young** professionals can take responsibility for bridging their communication styles and ways of engaging.

I wish I knew all of this when I first entered the workforce after college!

As a "Generation Yer" entering the workforce, or as some like to call it "entering the 'real world,'" I was eager to put my education and experience to work. Although my academic performance before college was less than stellar, I had taken the initiative and made the most of my opportunities in college. As a result, I had many great mentors and held a variety of leadership positions during six years of undergraduate and postgraduate study.

I had grown comfortable with the academic world, but I left that comfort behind to accept a fellowship with a federal agency in Washington, DC. While I had little clarity as to what I wanted to do with my career, I felt a deep need to show what I was capable of, find mentors and gain positive feedback for my contribution. As you can imagine, I was eager to plunge into the workforce and show them all what I was capable of achieving. Nevertheless, my managers interpreted these actions as my being overly needy or unwilling to "pay my dues." That was never my intention!

I could not understand why the seasoned professionals in my department ignored my enthusiasm or found it off-putting. I really thought I was demonstrating how much I wanted to help them — and the organization — succeed. Didn't they see that helping me would help them? Yet, I blew through five mentors and completed my fellowship with no idea of what I was going to do next.

After my fellowship, the first organization to offer me a position was a government contractor, and I took the job merely "because it was there." I started out doing qualitative research. I received high praise for my work and enjoyed it, but then got shifted over to meeting planning, which I found boring. After four months of planning meetings, I took the initiative and began reading every media document the company had put out during the 25 years it had been in business. After completing all my research, I presented my study to the head of the company.

My hope, of course, was that the CEO would recognize that I was capable of doing so much more, including building the business. Instead, she said, "Misti, what did your parents do to deal with you? It's clear you have problems with anxiety, do you take medication for that?"

> "With everything that has happened to you, you can either feel sorry for yourself or treat what has happened as a gift. Everything is either an opportunity to grow or an obstacle to keep you from growing. You get to choose."
>
> **WAYNE DYER**
> *Self-help advocate, author, and lecturer*

After all the time I spent working on understanding the business (in hopes of getting some new, more exciting work), she showed no interest and completely misinterpreted my actions. Without knowing where I was going or what I was going to do, I turned in my letter of resignation the next day.

I had moved across the country to Washington, DC, with huge expectations for both myself, and my employer. Yet here I was, jobless by choice, directionless and with no clear options. Lying on the floor of my one-bedroom apartment and truly worried about my future, I felt more lost and scared than I could ever properly express. Without first formulating a plan or building a network, I had just quit my job in a city where I knew practically no one *and* I had no career direction! I really didn't know where to begin.

I had a choice — I could stay on the floor and feel sorry for myself, or I could start making connections and begin learning about the possibilities "out there." Realizing that I needed to regain my focus and build a network that would open the future to me, I chose to make cold phone calls for the purpose of scheduling informational interviews.

> *"The few things that work fantastically well should be identified, cultivated, nurtured, and multiplied."*
>
> RICHARD KOCH
> *Author, management consultant*

Dedicating my time and energy to conducting informational interviews over the next several months, I also began researching generational differences because I *needed* to understand what had happened to me. During this exploration time, I heard many stories similar to my own from other young professionals who were also feeling directionless, nervous about their future and "disconnected" after leaving college. Like me, many were unclear about how to gain positive traction in their careers; they also had huge expectations of themselves and their employers.

I recognized the need to help other young professionals, as well as myself.

Six months later, after having completed over 150 informational interviews, I had done the field research to gain a clear understanding of what was happening between young and seasoned professionals. In addition, as I read published research on generational diversity, I realized, "Ah, I said this and they heard that."

I knew seasoned professionals wanted to help young professionals and vice versa — they simply didn't know how to communicate effectively with each other. So I started a new company — Inspirion, Inc. — to help companies create the systems that attract and retain talent across generations.

Now, after extensive research into generational diversity, personally witnessing both seasoned and young professionals struggle with the difference in their communication styles and coaching them through their challenges, I decided to write a book conveying critical, proven strategies that young professionals *and* seasoned professionals can use to truly bridge the generational gap.

Since I began Inspirion, I have had the privilege of speaking on generational diversity to thousands of people all over America and have worked directly with companies, executives and top military leaders to help them successfully manage the generational challenge so evident in today's workplace. I have received countless notes, emails and voice-mail messages from people telling me how understanding generational differences has had a huge impact on the way they communicate with professionals of varied generations. They no longer think, "That person is going about it all wrong." But rather, "Ah, I understand that is just a generational difference, now let's *refocus onto what matters most: our common vision.*"

In the pages that follow, I will share with you some of their stories and outline specific ideas and action steps you can begin using today for your organization, your team members and yourself to create the success you really desire, with every generation and at any level.

Moving forward takes diligence and desire, an understanding of the tools available and application of strategies that work. The result is increased productivity, motivation, inspiration, alignment and improvement to the bottom line, both individually and organizationally.

Let this book guide you throughout your career to bridge the intergenerational communication gap and assist you in becoming a more effective leader in your career today, and where you aspire to be tomorrow.

I wish you the best on your journey!

Misti Burmeister

1

"HOW DO I...?"

"How do I get them to care?" "How do I help them to be most productive?" "How do I help them understand they need to slow down?" "How do I get my team, from various generations, to work well together?" These are questions I am frequently asked by seasoned professionals.

Seasoned professionals want to understand how best to tap into and utilize the talents and skills of their staff, regardless of generation. Although seasoned professionals are often put off by their younger colleagues' impatience, communication style, appearance, etc., they want to know how to help them succeed.

According to a survey on job satisfaction conducted by leadership training and research company Leadership IQ, **the biggest driving force for Generation Y is praise and recognition**. This doesn't cost a thing — it's simply about leadership style. Managers have become used to catering to the needs of seasoned professionals whose driving factor, according to the survey, is a clear measure of their performance.

Additionally, it's important to note that **leaders lead people and managers manage projects.** People prefer to be led, rather than managed. Clearly, **leaders need to be flexible in their leadership style** in order to be most effective with all generations in the workplace.

In a white paper entitled *The Under-Management Epidemic,* Bruce Tulgan, the founder of RainmakerThinking, discusses the "Five Management Basics," in which he indicates the importance of offering:

· *Clear statements of performance requirements and standard operating procedures related to recurring tasks and responsibilities.*

· *Clear statements of defined parameters, measurable goals, and concrete deadlines for all work assignments for which the direct report will be held accountable.*

· *Accurate monitoring, evaluation, and documentation of work performance.*

· *Clear statements of specific feedback on work performance with guidance for improvement.*

· *Rewards and detriments distributed fairly.*

The paper states that only 25% of managers discuss the "Five Management Basics" with direct reports on a monthly basis; only 65% do it even once a year.

When leadership is not interacting with direct reports on these basic matters, it becomes impossible to create an environment where employees can flourish. While seasoned professionals may be accustomed to receiving clear, measured, formal performance feedback on a yearly or bi-annual basis, young professionals crave additional guidance, and with an expanding job market, they have the freedom to easily change companies in search of their "ideal" opportunity.

When I listen to young professionals share their ambitions, I know they will have difficulty being received well by most seasoned professionals. Walking into a seasoned professional's office making statements such as, "I want your job in the next six months," or "I want balance," or "Give me more opportunities," does not align a young professional with seasoned professionals — or the organization's vision/mission. On the other hand, if seasoned professionals understood what young professionals really mean when they say these sorts of things, they would be able to better harness that energy, rather than take the words as a personal attack (which I have seen many do).

Differences, when not understood, can cause conflict. Likewise, when differences are understood and highlighted as positive, newfound commonality is created and people work together more productively.

I have encountered many stories about seasoned professionals taking offense at the language of young professionals. They assign a meaning to the actions of young colleagues, or what they said because of *how* it was said, rather than simply **inquiring further** and perhaps **giving them feedback** on how they are coming across.

> "Good leadership consists in showing average people how to do the work of superior people."
> JOHN D. ROCKEFELLER
> (1839 — 1937)

You could ask something like, "What do you mean by that?" or "What is your anticipated timeframe for this to take place?" or "Would you explain in more detail?" This yields fertile ground for discussion and injects a dose of reality into the situation, creating understanding as to what the younger staff member really desires and what it will take to get there.

Alice, a young professional, went to her first meeting with her new supervisor, Joan, without pen and paper in hand. Joan, a seasoned professional assigned a lot of meaning to that one action/inaction (i.e. she doesn't respect me, she's not serious about her job, etc.).

When I asked Joan to consider other ways she could have interpreted Alice's actions, she had no idea what to say. I suggested that perhaps, based on her generation, the young woman simply didn't know she should arrive with a pen and paper ready to take notes, as no one ever told her. Alice, like so many in her generation, is used to being told exactly what to do, when to do it and how to do it. I asked Joan to consider the possibility that Alice *could* be the best employee she's ever had because she's so committed, talented and realize that she simply needs a little guidance.

Similarly, in my work with the sales team at a large telecommunications company, many seasoned professionals were agitated with the young professionals' inability to communicate personally with clients. They simply assumed their younger colleagues *should* have certain skill sets (after all, *they* did when they entered the workforce), and were disappointed and annoyed when a client expressed dissatisfaction.

Our colleges and universities produce bright graduates who are incredible with computers, enthusiastic in their approach to work and life and have a real desire for success. (Congratulations Baby Boomers — you taught them so well — they believe they can have, be and do anything they want!)

Yet according to a national study conducted by the American Institutes for Research, many young professionals are entering the workforce lacking skills that would allow them to use their knowledge more effectively. Many don't know how to set goals, create a career plan or budget their time or money. Their face-to-face communication skills are insufficient, and they don't know how to ask for help. Many fear they will come across as ignorant or somehow blameworthy if they ask for help, whether it be assistance in understanding the corporate culture, creating a plan or determining how best to communicate with their superiors.

> *"It has been my observation that most people get ahead during the time that others waste."*
>
> **HENRY FORD**
> *Founder, Ford Motor Company*

Focusing on proficiencies that young professionals "should have" *wastes time and energy* which could be more productively spent **helping them gain the skills** necessary to successfully carry out the organization's vision and mission. After all, isn't that task of paramount importance? If young employees are lacking in skills, help them create a plan to acquire what they are missing.

In most cases, helping a younger professional develop an important skill **will cost you nothing** more than a few minutes — the time it takes to think through the best strategy to impart that skill. The sales team I mentioned earlier found a way to help their young professionals build people-skills by having them attend in-person, client meetings with a skilled communicator (usually a seasoned professional).

My goal throughout this book is to offer solutions to such challenges. The real truth is that your young employees are all just beginning their career journey and need to continue developing themselves in order to help your organization continue to achieve great results. Even if they don't know how to ask for it, they need your help in learning important lessons in a way they can understand. Over time, with your assistance, young professionals will pick up the skills they need to succeed in your organization.

PRODUCTIVITY AND TEAMWORK

When it comes to productivity and getting a multi-generational team to work well together, what is most important is clarity and individual alignment with an organization's vision/mission. Many seasoned professionals have said to me, "What do you mean? I created a vision and mission, brought my team together and *told* them what we would be doing. They *should* know; *they* need to get on board." If leading people were that easy, we could all simply go around saying, "Be here at this time, do this work and stay until you're done."

> "Genuine leadership comes from the quality of your vision and your ability to spark others to extraordinary performance."
> JACK WELCH
> *Former General Electric Chairman and CEO*

Instead, I encourage you to bring your team together, share your vision and provide a space in which workers can contribute their ideas and create a mission together. (More on this in Chapter Five.)

As team members align with your vision, they create the mission and set major goals. Ask for volunteers to take on *responsibility* for the *results*. As individuals step up to the plate, you may think to yourself, "He/she cannot do this/that — they haven't been here long enough; they don't have enough training." I encourage you to let those conversations go and simply see what happens.

Be ready to coach your team along the way, as they will likely need your support. Young professionals are notorious for thinking they know how to do something simply because they read about it somewhere or have taken a class. Encourage this risk-taking and support it. There's no doubt they will have difficulties, but experiencing what author and leadership expert John C. Maxwell calls "failing forward" will be a valuable learning experience for young professionals.

As a leader, this is where you **let go of *how* employees reach their goals.** If they are hitting their targets, keeping the customers happy and contributing as team players, allow them creativity and autonomy. This kind of thinking requires a great deal of patience both with young professionals and with yourself.

There's absolutely nothing wrong with letting younger colleagues know your greatest concern is ensuring the customer is taken care of and that this new way of leading is pushing you out of your comfort zone. Lead by example and be willing to admit your discomfort. The truth is, there's room for every human being to grow. Those willing to say, "I'm not perfect" and admit to their human shortcomings, gain a great deal more respect and credibility than those always trying to cover their mistakes and show just how close to perfect they are.

> *"You'll come to see that a man learns nothing from winning. The act of losing, however, can elicit great wisdom."*
>
> **ALBERT FINNEY**
> *as Uncle Skinner in the film* A Good Year

Think about it for a moment. What kind of leader are you most attracted to? Those who pretend to be perfect, know everything and control processes, or those willing to admit their limitations and listen to your ideas?

CAPTURING ATTENTION

Capturing the attention of young professionals also can be a challenge. In a meeting with a potential client, I had the opportunity to learn about some difficulties they were having with their emerging leader program, which was in its inaugural year. As one might expect, the vast majority of program participants belong to Generations X and Y.

Six months into the year-long program, they were encountering disengaged participants. In fact, several participants were more than simply disengaged — they were outright rude to some of the instructors. Through my conversations with Jan, who headed up the effort, it became clear that participants saw this program as merely a box to be checked off in order to keep their careers moving forward, rather than valuable training.

I listened to a description of the program and its intended goals, and then began asking questions:

· *What was going well and not-so-well in the program?*

· *When do participants seem to be engaged?*

· *What do program managers think needs to be adjusted?*

The leaders had a great list of what was going really well and only a short list of what was not going well. What stuck out for me, however, was that participants seemed to like the program only when the instructor went out of his or her way to be engaging.

This naturally led me to share with my potential client the reality of this generation: They were raised on television, chat rooms, instant messaging and video games. They are used to being stimulated and expect it *now*, whether "it" is feedback, gratification or anything else!

As soon as I mentioned this, Jan (a Boomer) came back with, "It is not my job to keep them entertained!"

Her exclamation reminded me of the words of Bruce Tulgan, "[Generation Y] **is the most high maintenance workforce in the history of the world** ... " [Emphasis added]

Tulgan goes on to say, "The good news is **they're also the most savvy, capable, knowledgeable new generation of workers in history** ... They walk in with more information in their heads, more information at their fingertips — and, sure, they have high expectations, but they have the highest expectations first and foremost for themselves." [Emphasis added.]

As Jennifer Deal mentions in her book *Retiring the Generation Gap, How Employees Young and Old Can Find Common Ground*, "When there are too few people for the number of jobs available, employees can ask for more, and organizations have to offer more if they want to ***attract and*** *keep employees* — even relatively young, untrained employees." [Emphasis added.]

Finding a way to keep participants engaged, *even entertained,* will likely increase participation and add to your program's overall success. While the more seasoned generation is far more tolerant and adaptive, and its members will therefore participate regardless of presentation type, every generation wants to be stimulated and involved. The biggest difference between generations is their respective skill sets and their approach to problem solving — if you can offer a variety of courses and keep them engaged, you'll be effective across generations.

Likewise, finding a way to provide acknowledgement for achievements, training, flex-time, career counseling, mentorship programs and giving all generations a voice will likely increase participation and organizational success.

The vast majority of young professionals I have met, are searching for an employer that will fully utilize their skills, aid in their professional development, value them *and* their contributions, and help them understand how to advance in the organization. With an abundance of options, *of course* they will look for companies providing environments that will enable them to thrive.

U.S. Labor Department statistics have shown that more than 25 percent of all workers in the United States have been with their companies less than one year, and more than 33 percent less than two years. They also predict that the average Gen Y'er will hold between 10 and 14 jobs by age 38. These are staggering statistics, to be sure, and emphasize the need for companies to work on employee retention. **Young professionals truly *need a reason* to stay with your organization!**

Sarah Galbraith, young professional and Change Management Specialist at Raytheon, quoting Carolyn Martin, offers this insight:

· *Gen Y's know how to learn fast — if what they're learning is **meaningful** to the job and their career.*

· *They want feedback fast — because they don't want to wallow in mistakes.*

· *They want recognition for their accomplishments fast —*
because that motivates them to keep on contributing.

· *In other words, they want managers who really do the job of*
*managing. They **will** stay with organizations who provide*
them with great coaches and mentors.

· *Indeed, Gen Y's are demanding, but what they demand*
(training, feedback, direction, guidance, support, recognition)
will only make them more effective employees and leaders.

The chapters ahead offer ideas and strategies for retention of young professionals and provide specific action items to leverage the talents and skills of each generation. The *only* way to bridge the generational gap is to help members of all generations reach their goals and understand their contribution to your organization.

There are ideas and strategies to help seasoned professionals foster productivity across generations through sharing lessons (mentoring), build a strategy for success (coaching) and have fun along the way.

Seasoned professionals will discover strategies to enhance their own careers and create a strategic plan for the future. This is critical to providing seasoned professionals the mental space and energy to support their staff. When seasoned professionals know where their career is headed, they are much more actively engaged and interested in supporting young professionals.

If you, as a leader, have no real plan for your future, how can you expect to plan for the future of your employees or your organization? Leaders without their own plans have a difficult time empowering others. Even if you enjoy the position you are currently in and want to stay there for as long as possible, **there are always skills to be developed and experiences to gain**. Not only will your employees begin to thrive, rather than merely survive, you will be supporting your organization in preparing the next generation of leaders. As a leader, it begins with you!

REFLECTIONS
CHAPTER ONE

HIGHLIGHTS
CHAPTER ONE

**The biggest motivators for Generation Y
are praise and recognition.**

**For seasoned professionals, the driving factor
is a clear measure of their performance.**

**Leaders lead people; managers manage projects.
People prefer to be led, rather than managed.**

**Leaders need to be flexible in their leadership style in order
to be most effective with all generations in the workplace.**

Give feedback to young professionals on how they "come across."

**When young colleagues make statements that don't sit right
with you, inquire further as to their meaning or intention.**

**Meet with your direct reports a minimum of one time per week.
If you're leading via telephone and email, check in every day.**

**The biggest difference between generations is their
respective skill sets and approach to problem solving.**

**To increase participation and boost the organization's
overall success, find ways to provide training, flex-time,
career guidance and mentorship programs. Acknowledge
achievements and give employees of all ages a voice.**

**The majority of young professionals are searching for
a company that will fully use their skills, aid in their professional
development, value them and their contributions and help them
understand how to advance in the organization.**

FIVE SHIFTS TO
COMMON UNDERSTANDING

The vast majority of books and research on the topic of generational communication are targeted toward helping seasoned professionals attract, retain and motivate young professionals. It's almost as if the success or failure of communication between generations has been placed entirely on the shoulders of seasoned professionals.

Communication between people of different generations is a responsibility held by both young and seasoned professionals. In order for young professionals to gain the respect and experiences they are longing for, they must understand how best to communicate in the world of seasoned professionals. Likewise, seasoned professionals must learn the most effective ways to draw out the best in their young professionals.

Shortly after sending out a newsletter entitled "Pay Your Dues — Build Credibility," I received numerous emails from the young professionals on my listserv. With a new understanding of the language used by seasoned professionals, they wanted more information on how to collaborate and communicate effectively across generations. Young professionals have demonstrated genuine interest in knowing how to create working relationships with seasoned professionals.

Since beginning my work on bridging the communication gap in organizations, my experience has shown me countless times that **it's not *what you say* that gets what you want; rather, it's *how you say it.*** In addition, simply understanding the experiences that created each generation's worldview will aid greatly in shifting the conversation (inside our minds) away from "right" vs. "wrong" and toward our individual and organizational missions/goals.

When young professionals understand why seasoned professionals place great importance on certain things and learn how to think and act in harmony with their elders' worldview, they will become more effective communicators. Likewise, when seasoned professionals understand why young professionals see the world the way they do, they will more effectively tap into the talents and skills of the youngest generation.

Challenges arise because we all define "respect," "feeling valued," or "working hard" in different ways. **Taking the time to understand what people *really* mean when they make comments that upset you will help tremendously.** If you probe a little deeper and perhaps ask what was meant by the comment, you'll likely find the intention was not what you thought. When the focus in conversation is about "right" vs. "wrong," it is helpful to come back to the common ground between people.

The following chart, "Five Shifts to Common Understanding," shows the corresponding viewpoints of both young and seasoned professionals, with a focus on creating common ground in each example:

SEASONED PROFESSIONALS	COMMON GROUND	YOUNG PROFESSIONALS
1. Paying Your Dues	Building credibility / create a *path*	Wanting it all now
2. Making them just do the work	Creating a *learning* relationship	What can the company do for me?
3. Make them appreciate what has come before them	Creating and focusing on a common *vision*	Bucking the system
4. Be at work when you are needed	Company/individual mission and vision *alignment* / *Accountability* for results	Freedom and flexibility in my schedule
5. Adhere to the rules	Creating a common *strategy* to reach the vision / Acceptable *risk*	I can do it faster and better and I have fresh ideas

I will cover each of "Five Shifts" separately in the following five chapters.

When you or your team members are unclear as to the organization's direction or individual career goals, there's a much greater need to protect and covet rather than share and contribute. However, when there is alignment between your company/department mission and individual career goals, synergy results. Team members see how their contribution affects the whole and the conversation switches from "Why am I not getting what I want?" to "How can I further support my organization, while advancing my career?"

Is there alignment in your organization? **When alignment is present, coming back to common ground is easy.**

REFLECTIONS
CHAPTER TWO

HIGHLIGHTS
CHAPTER TWO

Communication between people of
different generations is a responsibility
held by both young and seasoned professionals.

It's not what you say that gets what you
want; rather, it's how you say it.

Understanding the experiences of each generation
will help shift the conversation away from
"right" vs. "wrong" and toward individual
and organizational missions/goals.

Take the time to understand what people really mean
when they make comments that upset you.

When there is alignment between your
company/department mission and individual
career goals, team members understand how their
contribution affects the whole and productivity increases.

BUILDING CREDIBILITY/ CREATING A PATH

SEASONED PROFESSIONALS	COMMON GROUND	YOUNG PROFESSIONALS
1. Paying Your Dues	Building credibility / create a *path*	Wanting it all now

YOUNG PROFESSIONALS

As a young professional, you may have a deep desire to move ahead quickly, have your views heard immediately and draw a high salary. Most young professionals were raised being told they can have, be and do anything. And you can! You simply need to allow the necessary time to build strong relationships and to discover what you truly enjoy doing. Unfortunately, most young professionals have been shown over and over again the beginning and end of a success story, without being shown the path to that success. The path is what will get you to your goal!

One college woman illustrates this well while speaking about her internship experience:

"Like many Generation Y'ers, I was eager to get my foot in the door and tackle big projects. I wanted to see what it was like to work with high profile clients and solve large, complex problems. Mainly, I sought the internship because I felt that I could gain valuable experiences for my eventual career in management consulting. However, I thought about the internship only as a stepping stone to my ultimate goal, as opposed to a generally valuable learning experience.

> *"Don't be afraid to give your best to what seemingly are small jobs. Every time you conquer one it makes you that much stronger. If you do the little jobs well, the big ones will tend to take care of themselves."*
>
> **DALE CARNEGIE**

"Early on in my internship, I was frustrated because I expected to work alongside top executives on projects with clients, thinking that these projects would offer me the most opportunity for learning and growth. Instead, I was working on projects that I thought had little importance, and little relevance to my career goals, such as online research and other office tasks. I expected such tasks, but I did not expect them to be the majority of my work at this company. (This is an experience that many of my classmates have also expressed as interns. I have learned that our expectations are not necessarily the reality.)"

One of the difficulties in this situation was that this young woman had made assumptions about the internship and experienced disappointment as a result. She hadn't communicated her desires or her goals, nor had she sought out ways to get those goals and desires met.

When young professionals feel they aren't moving ahead quickly enough or get the recognition they are so used to getting, an intolerable feeling of failure sets in and they often begin looking for a new job. While there's certainly nothing "wrong" with any of these desires (or in changing jobs), I would encourage young workers to give the situation some time and thought before jumping ship.

Take time to consider your career goals, share them with a trusted mentor and look for ways to reach your goals while supporting your organization/team. For example, if your desire is to be the lead on a major project and you have only been with the company a few months, you might consider what experiences you could gain to prepare yourself for success in such a project. **Ask your manager what experiences/skills are required of a project leader.**

Consider this: If you were responsible for the success of a project, wouldn't you want to ensure the right person, with the right skills and experiences, is on the job? Certainly you would! Demonstrating your ability with smaller, less visible tasks helps managers to see your capabilities and increases their comfort level in giving you more responsibility.

Once you share your career goals and define a strategy, look for ways to gain the experience necessary to build credibility. This may mean creating opportunities for yourself, or taking on projects outside your specific job duties. It may even be necessary to volunteer time to gain the experience you want or need.

If your goal is to stand above the crowd and build strong relationships with seasoned professionals, **change your language from "all about me" to "all about the organization."** Even if you don't like what you're doing and don't know what you want to do, when you show up consistently and look for ways to support your team/organization, you will be thought of as a reliable, hard working employee.

As you determine where you want to be professionally, your reputation as a reliable, hard-working employee will follow you. You never know, perhaps a current boss or colleague may know your future boss very well. You will also gain support from the seasoned professionals around you — they will help you get what you "suddenly" realize you want.

I highly encourage you to **stay focused on delivering more than you promise, building strong relationships and exploring what you want most.**

Taking time to find common ground will enhance relationships and company productivity.

SEASONED PROFESSIONALS

During a presentation in Washington, DC, Billy, a Generation Xer, shared his frustration with Generation Yers: "When I began my career, I wanted to show them what I was made of, get great experiences and get ahead quickly. After 15 years in the workforce, I can see why experience is so important — I have a completely different understanding of what it takes to be successful. I don't get these Generation Yers — they want to have it all without first gaining some life experience."

I looked at him a little dumbfounded. Was he mindful of what he'd said? Clearly, he was unaware of the irony in his intense judgment of others who were starting out in the exact same manner that he did! As the workshop continued, Billy gained a new level of understanding and patience once he saw that the next generation was not really much different from his own.

Take a moment and recall when you first entered the workforce. Can you relate to the desire to get ahead, gain experiences/exposure? When you do, it's less likely you will take the actions/inactions of younger professionals as a personal attack. Instead, you may be able to **find a way to offer the experiences they are seeking while also reaching your individual and organizational goals.**

While many seasoned professionals can relate to the desire to gain experiences/exposure early, they can't understand the extreme level of impatience present in many young professionals today. I encourage you to stay in touch with that desire to move ahead, **stay focused on your mission, and help them understand how they can contribute.**

You might also encourage them to create a three-year plan, outlining both the skills they want to gain and the position they want to achieve. Their desire for skill level enhancement may fit very well into helping your organization reach its goals — it's a win/win. (You can access a three-year goal setting chart at *www.inspirioninc.com.*)

~ WITH A CAREER PLAN COMES PERSPECTIVE ~

During my presentations and speeches on generational diversity, I have heard many seasoned professionals express their frustration with the younger generation's constant need to move up before they have "proven themselves." "They need to pay their dues before asking for a promotion," these experienced workers say. "They haven't even been here a year yet!"

When today's seasoned professionals were entering the workforce, there were few career options. They took what they could and worked hard to prove themselves in order to get ahead. Today's young professionals leave school with an abundance of options, minimal job experience (over-planned lives didn't allow part-time work while in school) and great expectations.

Because many of them have been raised on media and in educational systems which told them exactly what to think, what to like/dislike, where to be and when to be there, they haven't had a chance to explore such concepts for themselves. So, with no real notion of what they really like, what they are naturally good at or what they want, they have high expectations — not only of their employer, but also of themselves. Imagine the pressure they must feel!

Additionally, with the media showing the beginning and end to success stories, but not the process it took to get there, they honestly think they can, and should, have it all right now. Imagine the frustration when they realize the time and consistent effort required to get the results they long for!

Even more daunting is that, **according to former Secretary of Education Richard Riley, "the top 10 jobs that will be in demand in 2010 didn't even exist in 2004. We are currently preparing students for jobs that don't yet exist ... using technologies that haven't yet been invented ... in order to solve problems we don't even know are problems yet."**

Both mentoring *and* coaching are extremely valuable and effective among the youngest generation. Simply put, **mentoring is about sharing your own life's lesson**, what's worked well/not-so-well for you. **Coaching is about asking questions to help them determine what might work best for them.** While they may choose similar career goals as you, the route they use to achieve them may be vastly different.

I assume you want to create loyalty among young professionals, help your organization retain talent, and become a natural/effective leader across generations. Therefore, I encourage you to begin asking your team hard questions that will help them identify their strengths and interests, and start developing a two- to three-year career plan. (You'll find a career-planning chart at *www.inspirioninc.com*.)

Starting with an understanding of likes and dislikes, developing a long-term career plan for each of your employees will help you each understand what experiences and skills are needed for career success. In addition, when employees are clear about the company's direction, they can more easily align themselves with its vision and mission. Without this alignment, your employees will remain grossly under-utilized.

Please note: You can only ask of your employees what you are willing to do yourself. Before requesting that they create a plan, go through the process yourself. (See Chapter Thirteen for more information on creating a plan.)

Jim, a seasoned professional and vice president for a major electric company, mentioned his frustration with helping young professionals create a plan for their future. "When I first came into the workforce, I set my mind to rising up in the organization and did what was necessary to get the promotions I wanted. Today, when I ask my young professionals what position they would like to get into down the road, they look at me a little funny and rarely have an answer. When they do have an answer, they are less willing than I was to relocate in order to take the promotion. It seems they prefer to stay near their family and are unwilling to make adjustments to ensure their success or the organization's success. I don't want to retire until I have set my people and company up for success. How do I help them with their careers and develop the leadership for my company?"

It's true that most young professionals are not thinking long-term, for themselves or the organization. They are focused on the day and, if you're lucky, the week. However, like professionals of all generations, they want to be successful. The following are a list of questions I encouraged Jim to ask his young professionals.

- *Where do you see yourself in five years?*

- *What skills do you most enjoy using?*

- *What experience would you like to gain?*

- *What skills would you like to develop?*

- *What do you like most about working for this organization?*

- *If you could see any change in this organization, what would it be?*

- *Do you see yourself as an important part of this organization?*

- *Would you like to lead people?*

- *In which areas do you need to develop in order to get into the position you most want?*

- *Are you willing to relocate? What are your parameters for relocating?*

- *How do you prefer to be managed?*

- *How can I best help you to reach your potential?*

> *"The essence of leadership is not giving things or even providing visions. It is offering oneself and one's spirit."*
>
> **LEE BOLMAN & TERENCE DEAL**

Be prepared for a whole bunch of "I don't knows," as many younger workers haven't thought about their experiences or their future in this way. **Keep asking the questions and request that they spend time thinking about the answers.** If they are having difficulty, ask them to take three questions home with them and set a follow-up meeting to discuss the issue further. Asking these questions will be help them find direction and it also lets them know you care about their future. *This* is how you create the loyalty that SO many organizations and leaders are seeking. Yes, you *must* put time and energy into developing your talent.

The truth is that you do care about their future! **When employees' interests are in alignment with your company's vision and mission, everyone wins.** When they clearly understand the organization's vision/mission and see how they contribute it, they are more likely to fully participate in the workplace and perhaps gain clarification about their professional goals.

REFLECTIONS
CHAPTER THREE

HIGHLIGHTS
CHAPTER THREE

YOUNG PROFESSIONALS

Take time to consider your career goals
and share them with a trusted mentor.

Look for ways to reach your goals while
supporting your organization/team.

Ask your manager what experiences/skills
are required of a project leader.

Demonstrating your ability with smaller tasks, helps
managers to see your capabilities and increases their
comfort level in giving you more visible, larger projects.

Shift your language from "all about me"
to "all about the organization."

Stay focused delivering more than you promise, building
strong relationships and exploring what you want most.

SEASONED PROFESSIONALS

Find a way to offer the experiences young
professionals are seeking, while also reaching
your individual/organizational goals.

Stay focused on your vision/mission and help young
professionals understand how they can contribute.

Encourage young professionals to create
a three-year plan, outlining both the skills they want
to gain and the position they want to achieve.

WITH A CAREER PLAN COMES PERSPECTIVE

Mentoring is about sharing your own life's lesson,
what's worked well/not-so-well for you.

Coaching is about asking questions to help an individual
determine what might work best for them.

Ask young professionals strategic questions and request
they spend time thinking about the answers.

When interests are in alignment with
the mission, everyone wins.

NOTE: Goal setting and career planning charts
are available at *www.inspirioninc.com.*

CREATING A
LEARNING RELATIONSHIP

SEASONED PROFESSIONALS	COMMON GROUND	YOUNG PROFESSIONALS
2. Making them just do the work	Creating a *learning* relationship	What can the company do for me?

Jackie, a seasoned lawyer, shared a story about a young colleague. Jason had been with the law firm for a couple of years and had recently tendered his letter of resignation. When Jackie asked Jason to help her understand why he was leaving, he responded, "I'll do as many client dinners as you would like, but this office work is not for me."

Jason clearly didn't understand the big picture perspective of how to contribute to the firm's success. Being a lawyer in a firm means that **you are a part of a team** — a team that serves customers. Everyone must do their part so the customers receive great service. While dinner with clients or potential clients is a great way to develop/strengthen relationships, it's only the icing on the cake. What's most important is a job well done!

Consider this: If your hair stylist provided great conversation — and a lousy haircut — would you go back? Probably not! Conversation and relationship building are important. Yes, people do buy from those they like. Nevertheless, **keeping clients and getting great referrals depends on client satisfaction above all else.**

While you may not enjoy all tasks set before you, they are a necessary part of the business. If no one does them, the customer will not be properly taken care of. Remember, **your customers keep you employed — without them, no one in your company has a job.** Take a step back to see the bigger picture and look for ways to contribute to your team/organization's success. This will help you build a great reputation for both yourself and your company. Eager and helpful employees get promoted!

If you're clear about your career goals, **look for ways to align your objectives with those of your organization.** If you are unclear about them, use this time to test out different opportunities. Ask questions about your job and the possibilities for advancement. Once you understand what's available to you, you can better determine your goals and request direction from your supervisors.

> *"It is literally true that you can succeed best and quickest by helping others to succeed."*
>
> NAPOLEON HILL

Attitude is everything. Do what needs to be done without complaining. Be patient. Consistently communicate your career aspirations with the right people. And do what's necessary for the success of the company. These are the actions of people who rise to the top of organizations. Over time, you, too, will be noticed and promoted.

By the way, the "right people" to share your career aspirations with are your supervisor and those in a position to help you advance. Look for ways to help these people *and* share your aspirations along the way. Always look for win/win opportunities!

SEASONED PROFESSIONALS

During the one year I worked at a federal agency, I was assigned five different Baby Boomer mentors, one after another. I was looking forward to gaining direction and additional contacts from mentoring meetings, but each mentor sent me out the door with plenty of work, but no direction. I left the meetings frustrated and confused. What I really needed was assistance with creating my career path and understanding how the work I was doing fit into the bigger organizational picture.

It wasn't until I began doing research on generational differences that I came to understand my experiences. Baby Boomers grew up during a time when choices were in short supply and the focus was on "working hard" and "making a good impression" to get ahead. In their world, once you got a job you put your head down and got to work, because that was your company until you retired. Obedience and loyalty were rewarded.

Today's young professionals have an abundance of choices and little direction. Many young professionals don't see how doing a great job with small projects demonstrates their abilities and sets them up for opportunities to tackle bigger projects. If they don't have access to highly visible projects right away, many consider themselves failures.

Helping young workers better understand their strengths, create a career plan and see how their career plan fits into the company's vision/mission will increase the likelihood of success for them, for you and for the organization. With this understanding, they will be more inclined to work hard, stay focused and remain with your company.

Take, for example, the intern's story from Chapter Three. Her manager's initial thoughts were that, "She has expressed a desire to be included on 'high-powered' projects, yet her actions haven't demonstrated that desire. I cannot bring her into confidential meetings with potential or existing clients without first being certain that she has a firm commitment to the company and a solid understanding of our vision/mission. I need to be certain that she's willing to do what's necessary to get the experiences she says she desires."

The manager assured me that, "Without question, this intern is an incredibly talented young woman ... . *And* her talents really show up when she applies herself. My perception is that, as a result of her multiple involvements, everything she does gets muted attention."

This is a common scenario with young professionals. They have a busy schedule and a broad range of experiences with no real in-depth understanding, yet they think they have it mastered all.

During a meeting where they both opened themselves to growth, the leader and intern were able to find common ground. They realized they had each been making assumptions, rather than communicating their goals and concerns. They resolved to communicate more regularly and to question their assumptions. The intern expressed her goals and desires, and the leader discussed ways that at least some of those desires could be attained.

As a result of their willingness to dig deep and communicate their issues, the intern has demonstrated dramatic improvements with regard to following through with her commitments and being accountable. She also discovered that she's learning more than she had anticipated from this internship, and in different areas than she originally expected.

After this bit of improvement on the part of the intern, a gap still remained between what she said she wanted and her actions. One of her requests was to attend an important meeting with a potential high-powered client. The leader was reticent to agree, but the intern's direct supervisor encouraged the leader to reconsider. The leader eventually agreed provided that the intern complete certain preparations within a specific timeframe. To everyone's surprise, the intern fulfilled the criteria superbly, attended the meeting and gave an exceptional presentation to the potential client.

Your organization's long-term success depends on its young professionals. Even more than taking the time to mentor and coach them, be willing to take risks with them. Their competence may surprise you!

~ CREATING A LEARNING
ENVIRONMENT — A TRUE STORY ~

When Veronica first came to ABC Company as a part-time executive assistant, it was clear that she had great potential. *However*, she was usually late, was very focused on getting the experiences *she* wanted, and never mentioned a long-term interest in being a part of ABC Company. While she did an excellent job with the tasks her CEO, Melissa, gave her, she never took the initiative to look beyond the scope of her work for additional ways to be of value to ABC.

When Veronica was hired, she made a verbal commitment for one year. This allowed Melissa to focus on growing ABC, as she knew her new hire would take care of administrative tasks for her.

About a month into Veronica's tenure, she told Melissa she was looking for another job and would only be with the company another week or two. Though Melissa was, as you can imagine, very upset and irritated, she knew that focusing on her anger would do no good. Instead, she expressed her disappointment regarding the one-year commitment, and wished Veronica well in finding her calling.

Then, something changed. While Veronica never said directly to Melissa that she wanted to stay, she kept showing up every Friday as previously agreed. After a few weeks, Melissa asked if she could expect her to stay around. Veronica said she was recommitted.

> *"Great ability develops and reveals itself increasingly with every new assignment."*
> BALTASAR GRACIAN

With a sigh of relief, Melissa became more committed to offering Veronica the experiences desired (face time with clients). She had skills Melissa didn't have and an engaging personality; she simply needed coaching and mentoring.

For example, rather than harping about Veronica's punctuality, Melissa focused on results and on giving her employee clear expectations. As long as the work was getting done and Veronica showed up to important meetings on time, Melissa let the rest take care of itself. This was in spite of the fact that on more flexible days, she was between 30 minutes to a couple of hours late for work. (As author/educator Jonathan Kozol said, "Pick battles big enough to matter, small enough to win.")

About eight months into Veronica's part-time assistance, Melissa began to think about hiring someone full-time to help her grow ABC. While Melissa really enjoyed working with Veronica, her assistant was spread thin working full-time for her family business, plus juggling friends, school and personal challenges. Her timeliness had improved, but she was still on the periphery of the company.

But one day Veronica suddenly began looking for ways to help grow ABC. Two changes seemed to spawn this shift: First, Melissa brought on a new intern (giving Veronica both an associate, as well as more responsibility than the new co-worker). Second, she began helping Veronica develop an appreciation for the company's vision and mission (i.e. aligning her with the company's vision/mission). Melissa also made sure Veronica understood her value to the long-term success of ABC (i.e., acknowledgement).

Veronica began taking workshops on building businesses. Her energy was contagious and Melissa began to think about how her employee could become more involved in her overall vision for the company. Melissa talked with Veronica about her strengths and offered her a leadership role with regard to the intern.

The more responsibility Melissa gave Veronica, the more effort she devoted to the business. Before long, she came to Melissa with a clear need. Her family business was shutting down for the season and she needed full-time work. While Melissa wasn't certain she was ready to hire someone full time, she decided that the value Veronica brought to the company made it worth taking the leap.

Not only did Melissa hire Veronica full-time, she also promoted her to business manager. Every day Veronica demonstrates her commitment to the company's mission/vision. She is now a key person in the firm and over time will likely become a partner.

Here's what Veronica said about her process:

When I began at ABC, I had come from a job where I had worked hard, felt unappreciated and saw others receive promotions and benefits from my work instead of me. This left me with little motivation to contribute.

I considered working at ABC because Melissa was offering "coaching," which, to me meant some sort of guidance; something I completely lacked in my last job. Still, in my mind, I was merely exchanging administrative work for coaching, plus a small salary. I saw no need to contribute more, even though I knew how.

Concerning the "magic change": Melissa helped my self-esteem. Because I heard her commending my work and character to others, I knew she wasn't just thanking me to keep me working, but truly believed her statements. She has made sure to let me know that my opinions and suggestions are always appreciated (whether used or not), which has, in turn, made it easier for me to keep an open mind to her ideas. Learning about self-growth and affirmations, and coaching me through small problems, made me feel like she cared about my success as well as the company's. One of Melissa's sayings is that if I'm not taking care of myself, I can't really take care of our company.

She taught me accountability. As a result, I began making a conscious effort to be on time and even read a few books on time management to learn how to improve that area of my life.

Part of the coaching process was also to help me learn how to 'run my own business.' While I was successful in keeping a business running, I was not great at gaining new clients, building relationships or networking.

Hearing Melissa re-affirming the mission of the company day in and day out, really made me see how I contribute to the mission. Letting me grow within my position and taking the bar to new heights, lets me know that I'm in charge of how far I can grow within ABC and that I have her support in creating my career.

Veronica and Melissa have developed a foundation of trust and a common vision. They also have grown to care a great deal about one another's success. In making her own mistakes, Melissa knows she can be vulnerable with Veronica. Veronica has watched Melissa fall flat on her face, then pick herself up again and keep on going. Truly, Veronica has taught Melissa at least as much as Veronica has taught her. That's what makes them a great team — the team they had to become to grow ABC.

REFLECTIONS
CHAPTER FOUR

HIGHLIGHTS
CHAPTER FOUR

YOUNG PROFESSIONALS

Being an employee in a company means that you are a part of a team — a team that serves customers. Everyone must do their part so the customer receives great service.

Keeping clients and getting great referrals depends on client satisfaction above all else.

Look for ways to align your goals with your organization's goals.

Ask questions about your job and how to advance within your organization.

Attitude is everything: Follow the actions of people who rise to the top inside your organization.

SEASONED PROFESSIONALS

Help young professionals:
· Develop a greater understanding of their own strengths
· Create a career plan and see how their career plan fits into the vision/mission of your company (See the big picture.)
· Gain the necessary experience to set them up for success

Your organization's long-term success depends on the success of its young professionals.

Even more than taking the time to mentor and coach younger workers, be willing to take risks with them. Their competence may surprise you!

CREATING A
COMMON VISION

SEASONED PROFESSIONALS	COMMON GROUND	YOUNG PROFESSIONALS
3. Make them appreciate what has come before them	Creating and focusing on a common *vision*	Bucking the system

YOUNG PROFESSIONALS

According to Boston-based research company, the Aberdeen Group, **90 percent of employees make the decision to stay at a company within the first six months.** Whether this is "right" or "wrong," it is a fact that should keep both organizations and employees on their toes.

Here is how this "stay or go" decision process played out with one young professional:

Ken, a young professional at a large telecommunications company and a previous coaching client of mine, had been with his company for five years. He wanted to be promoted sooner; he also wanted to be more involved in higher level management decision making. His company, like many companies this size, had a very specific system for promotion and Ken did not yet meet the criteria for advancement. As a result, he didn't make the pay he felt he deserved, nor could he get involved in top-level meetings.

Ken went out of his way, attempting to break through the promotion system in order to gain the opportunities and salary he wanted. After six months of running into roadblocks and red tape, Ken gave up and took a job with another company. Instead of sticking it out, building relationships and looking for ways to be of service to his company, he quit.

Within the first two months, Ken called to let me know he wasn't happy in his new position. He realized that he had jumped ship too soon and wanted coaching on how to approach his previous employer to be rehired. He also wanted to learn about the value of established systems.

In a *BusinessWeek* article (May 28, 2007) entitled "Which Job is the Right Job?" Jack and Suzy Welch point out that, "There are five questions you need to ask yourself as you weigh competing opportunities: Will the new job be filled with co-workers who share my sensibilities, or will I have to zone out or fake it to get along? Will the new job stretch my mind and build my skills, and otherwise take me out of my comfort zone, or am I entering at the top of my game? Will the new job open or close doors for me should I ever leave? Will the new job turn my crank, touch my soul, and give me meaning? Who am I making happy by taking this job, and am I OK with that bargain?"

Needless to say, Ken neglected to ask himself these important questions before he jumped ship. We all have our own lessons to learn and Ken clearly learned his. **Individuals who stay around and demonstrate commitment to the mission and vision of the organization are likely to be promoted.**

On the other hand, some promotional systems do need updating to meet with changing times. Established law firms offer a good example of outdated systems. Once a young lawyer begins working for a firm, they must wait six to nine years to be offered a partnership position. There are no intermediate steps to denote accomplishments. Waiting six to nine years to get to the next level is longer than many young lawyers care to wait.

Rebecca Logan echoes this in her article "Making Partner Can Be a Trade-Off for Lawyers" (*Washington Business Journal,* June 8-14, 2007). "Nowadays, these kids are coming into our offices … saying, 'I really want to work on this' or 'I didn't get that kind of work over the last three months.' They're much more proactive — or paranoid — about managing their careers."

Today's young professionals are used to being consistently rewarded for their accomplishments. This is neither "right" nor "wrong" — it just *is*. Adding levels provides a way to promote and recognize your people. Opportunities for promotion recognize achievements and recognition is the number one thing young professionals are seeking.

When organizations create more steps on the career ladder and greater opportunities for acknowledgement and rewards, including levels of accomplishment, they often see an increased retention among their young professionals.

SEASONED PROFESSIONALS

Steve, a master chief in the Navy, told me this story when I was speaking on a Navy "road show" in San Diego:

One of Steve's direct reports, Frank, let him know that a young sailor, Josh, would not wash the dishes in the specific way that was required. Steve said, "What do you mean he won't do the dishes that way?" Frank replied, "That's it. He said he won't do the dishes." So, Steve went to Josh to inquire further.

Steve approached Josh and asked him why he wouldn't wash the dishes in the required manner. The young sailor said, "This sign here tells us how to wash the dishes and the chief says to do it differently, and that makes no sense." Steve responded, "What the chief says to do is the right way to wash the dishes, but what you're telling me is having that sign posted makes no sense, right?" Josh proudly exclaimed, "Yep, it makes no sense!"

Steve looked at the sign and agreed with the young sailor, "You're right, having that sign there makes no sense." Then he went on to say, "Now that we are in agreement regarding the sign, would you also agree with me that the dishes still need to be done, regardless of this stupid sign?" Josh looked at Steve and said, "Yes, the dishes still need to be done." Steve left and Josh began doing the dishes.

Steve stopped to fully listen to what was upsetting Josh, acknowledged his frustration without telling him he was wrong and got him focused on the mission at hand, the dishes. Sometimes people just need to be acknowledged and understood, then refocused. In this case, Steve and Josh created the alignment of a common vision, thereby allowing matters to move forward.

While on the surface it may seem that someone is "bucking the system," it may actually be that they are either confused and need more direction, or have an idea that is worth listening to.

Simply pushing someone into what you want them to do is only going to cause frustration and conflict. When you meet frustration with frustration and seek to gain control, what you get is even more frustration. Likewise, when you meet frustration with compassion and listening — even when the other person seems "wrong" — you transform the energy in a positive direction and the situation can move forward.

APPRECIATING THE PAST, PREPARING FOR THE FUTURE

While we aren't addressing gender-related issues in this book, it's worthwhile to note that as young women enter the workforce, many seasoned female professionals want to be acknowledged and appreciated for all they endured to gain opportunities for women. This is a frequent challenge among seasoned women professionals.

> *"Courage is what it takes to stand up and speak; courage is also what it takes to sit down and listen."*
> WINSTON CHURCHILL

The biggest problem is that young professionals don't know what came before and don't *understand* what women went through to accomplish the current climate for women in the workplace. Many of today's young professionals grew up with both parents working and were, to a greater extent than ever before, "raised" by institutions, each other and the media. They don't have a clear understanding of the experiences of the women who came before them. This has both advantages and disadvantages.

The advantage is that young workers **have a fresh set of eyes and are able to recognize process improvements and opportunities that may not be obvious to seasoned professionals**. They are anxious to try new approaches and make a mark for themselves. The disadvantage is that they do not know what has already been tried, what has worked well, what has not, and why.

Helping young professionals to understand the progression of established systems, and being open to hearing their ideas for possible improvements is a great way to create common ground. Sometimes current processes need to remain as they are and sometimes they need to be revamped to reflect current technologies,

> *"Vision must be defined by the leader. But it is the subordinates who must define the objectives that move the organization toward the desired outcome."*
> LT. GEN. WILLIAM G. PAGONIS

market changes, etc. What's most important is to communicate a clear mission, based on an understanding of the organization's vision, and move forward with ideas and innovations.

Whether you're a seasoned or young professional, your flexibility, communication and understanding will go a long way toward creating common ground.

~ WHAT ARE VISION/MISSION? ~

Leaders create the vision, which gives the long-term goal of where they, the team and the organization are headed.

A mission is a statement of purpose put together by a team of people, which creates clarity, focus, teamwork, personal accountability and inspiration. It gives direction as to how the vision will be achieved. Bringing key people together to strategize on your mission naturally creates synergy, teamwork and collaboration.

For example, here are Inspirion Inc.'s Vision and Mission:

Vision: Inspirion Inc. will know that it is being successful when people of different generations support and help each other regardless of differences.

Mission: To create generational partnerships throughout the world.

As you can see, the mission is the path (created by the team) to establish the vision (created by the leader). It's then up to the team and the leader, together, to determine the tasks that will enable the mission to be accomplished and the vision to be realized.

WHY CREATE A VISION/MISSION?

Imagine for a moment, a football team without a coach; a hockey team that doesn't know which net belongs to which team or an orchestra without a conductor. In each situation seriously under-utilized talent will set the stage for plenty of chaos, not to mention unhappy patrons!

When you and your team have clear instructions for hitting the target, you're more likely to reach your goal and increase your bottom line while leaving customers ecstatic.

If you want your team/organization focused, inspired, working together and taking personal responsibility, bring them together, create a mission statement and help them see how they each contribute to the success of that mission. This prevents them from drifting in different directions, perhaps at cross-purposes with one another, and not utilizing their abilities. **With a clear vision/mission, your team can consistently come together and determine what adjustments are necessary to move closer to their target.**

When organizations take the time to look at the big picture and create a meaningful mission and clear vision, those working for the organization naturally feel a sense of purpose in their work. When they clearly understand where the company is headed and the importance of their contribution toward accomplishing the vision, they naturally feel a sense of ownership.

WHO SHOULD CREATE THE VISION/MISSION?

Regardless of organization size or number of people on any given team, any person in a leadership position can pull their employees together to create a mission for the team that will be aligned with the vision. While the leader sets the tone, generates the energy and may be the person who calls and leads the meeting, **it's the team who creates the mission and the leader who creates the vision.**

TIPS ON CREATING THE VISION/MISSION?

Creating a great mission statement has to do with the energy/excitement generated within the team. I've heard mission statements that sound similar to this, "Make a billion dollars." While that may be a great goal, it isn't a mission that excites most young professionals. If your young professionals were promised a percentage of those dollars, they might get excited … but only momentarily.

A vision/mission should be something so empowering that individuals on the team are excited to do their best every day. Example: "Vision: To be the number one manufacturing company in the world, dedicated to employee development, customer satisfaction and community development. Mission: We are a company who listens and responds to the needs of our employees, our customers and our community."

Some questions to consider when creating a vision/mission:

· *What problem(s) do you solve? What need(s) do you fill?*

· *What do you sell? How do you make your money?*
  What is your revenue model?

· *How is your organization different from every other organization out there? What is your organization's unique selling proposition?*

· *Who do you sell to? What is your target market?*

· *What are your economic/financial goals?*

· *What are your social/community goals?*

· *What type of organization/team do you want to create?*
  Are you a "lifestyle" or "high potential" organization?

- *Where is the organization/team going?*
  What products/services/industries do you plan to venture into?

- *What is your five-year strategy? Do you want to sell
  internationally, build an online store, franchise your business,
  build certain partnerships, develop additional products?*

- *What are strengths/weaknesses of your team? What skills need
  to be strengthened? What talent needs to be brought in?*

I facilitated a mission/vision exercise for a team within a large telecommunications company. The result was increased teamwork, a renewed excitement for the future and a new sense of creativity and fun. Here's specifically what I did:

I first shared a short video demonstrating that regardless of where you work or what you do, you can make a contribution and create a legacy for yourself. In the video, a woman had recently taken over as CEO of a large grocery store chain. She gave a speech to her entire team to inspire and help them understand their importance toward the company's long-term success. She asked each of them to find their own unique way of creating a positive experience for their customers.

One young man, a bagger, took her request seriously and began creating his own unique way of touching each shopper. He found an inspiring quote each day and brought it typewritten on small pieces of paper. He would then place the little quote inside one grocery bag of each customer. Over time, customers would literally stand and wait in his line, even if the other registers were open, in order to receive his quote of the day.

Through her vision, the CEO was able to inspire her team toward a clear mission and allowed them the freedom to create their own unique contribution. Regardless of your position, you can always have a positive effect on the people around you, add value to your team and develop a first-class reputation.

After showing the video, I asked the team leader to identify his company's customers. Then I asked each individual to consider their own unique contribution to both the team and their customers. Finally, I had them brainstorm about the specifics of what they do and the value their team brings to the company. Within an hour, they created their team mission.

HOW DO YOU CONTRIBUTE TO
YOUR ORGANIZATION'S VISION/MISSION?

Once they had created their team mission statement, I asked each of them to think about their talents and what they most wanted to achieve in their careers. Because many of them had never thought about this, they wrote down the parts of their jobs they most enjoyed. *What do you love about what you are doing? Or what would you like to do?*

Next, they considered what job would allow them to focus on those most pleasurable tasks. This exercise gave them the framework for their career future. *What are your goals? Where do you want to be in the next three to five years? What new skills do you want to develop?*

I asked them to share their career goals and consider ways they could help each other reach these goals. *What relationships do you need to cultivate in order to achieve your goals?* While creating clarity, they were also able to see how they could support each

> *"A clear vision, backed by definite plans, gives you a tremendous feeling of confidence and personal power."*
> **BRIAN TRACY**
> *Author and Speaker*

other in gaining the experiences necessary to achieve their professional aspirations. A sense of teamwork and focus emerged that continues today. In fact, this team became more innovative in the following six months than they had been in years, and the company's sales have increased as a result.

If you want your team working *together* toward a common goal, you have to take the necessary time to create a mission *together* that is aligned with both your vision and the company's vision.

As demonstrated in the example above, once you create a clear vision/mission, the next step is to learn about the career interests of those on your team. Understanding each individual's goals and career aspirations is tremendously helpful toward best supporting them as individual contributors. Most people aren't really conscious of their abilities. Over time, and with your consistent support, their awareness will increase and you, as a leader, will gain tremendous loyalty as a result.

Confirming the critical nature of getting to know your team members, Thomas J. DeLong, et. al., wrote in their article entitled "Why Mentoring Matters in a Hypercompetitive World," (*The Harvard Business Review,* January 2008*)*, "Ask an associate what kind of work she wants to do, where her passions lie, what skills she wants to develop. Don't leave this important job to human resources."

When individual career aspirations are in alignment with your organization's vision/mission, synergy occurs. When the organization can provide opportunities for employees to gain the experiences they want, it's a win/win situation. This kind of alignment provides rich ground for individuals to perform at their best, while the organization prospers significantly.

The vision/mission should be readdressed every four to six months and more often as team members join and leave. There's huge value in consistently reestablishing the direction and re-empowering your team. For example, "[Simply Audio Books] also hosts monthly all-staff meetings to ensure employees are kept apprised of the company's strategic direction and how they fit into the pursuit of corporate goals. Equally important is helping young workers find a career path." (Jennifer Myers, "The How and the Y," *Profit Guide*, October 2007.)

The direction provided by the creation and recreation of a vision/mission is the foundation for any team's/organization's success.

REFLECTIONS
CHAPTER FIVE

HIGHLIGHTS

CHAPTER FIVE

YOUNG PROFESSIONALS

90% of employees make the decision to stay
at a company within the first six months.

Moving from company to company isn't necessarily
going to bring the results you seek.

Individuals who stay around and demonstrate
commitment to the mission and vision of the
organization, will likely get promoted.

When law firms and other companies create
more opportunities for recognition and rewards,
including levels to be reached, it is likely they will
see an increased retention of their young professionals.

SEASONED PROFESSIONALS

Flexibility, communication and understanding will
go a long way toward creating common ground.

While on the surface, it may seem that someone
is "bucking the system," it may actually be that they
are either confused and need more direction,
or have an idea that is worth listening to.

Communicate a clear vision and then, as a team,
create the strategy (mission) for getting there together.

When you meet frustration with compassion and listening (even when the other person seems "wrong") you transform the energy in a positive direction and the situation can move forward. Help young professionals understand the reasoning behind current processes and then listen to their ideas for possible improvements. They have a fresh set of eyes and are often able to recognize process improvements and opportunities that may not be obvious to seasoned professionals.

CREATING A VISION/MISSION

The vision states the long-term goal of where you, the team and the organization are headed and it is created by the leader.

A mission is a statement of purpose put together by a team of people, which creates clarity, focus, teamwork, personal accountability and inspiration. It gives the direction on how the vision will be achieved.

With a clear vision/mission, your team can consistently come together and determine what adjustments are necessary to get closer to their target.

A vision/mission should be something so empowering that the individuals on the team are excited to do their best every day.

The vision/mission should be readdressed every four to six months, and more often as team members join or leave.

ACCOUNTABILTY
FOR RESULTS

SEASONED PROFESSIONALS	COMMON GROUND	YOUNG PROFESSIONALS
4. Be at work when you are needed	Company/individual mission and vision *alignment* / *Accountability* for results	Freedom and flexibility in my schedule

YOUNG PROFESSIONALS

I have heard many young professionals say they are most interested in finding a company that provides them with freedom and flexibility. Jessica, a young professional, shared her interest in finding a job that would allow her to work when she is at her best (in the afternoon and evening). Once she found an organization where she could achieve her career goals, the scheduling seemed less important.

If you desire freedom and flexibility in your schedule, look for win/win situations. If it's possible to complete your work from home, or at a time when you are most productive, consider how you might approach your supervisor. The fact is that many people have a specific vision of how, when and where work is done. Many seasoned professionals need to see you in the office to know you are working. Not every leader sees the world the same way their employees do.

Take time to consider your leader's concerns, i.e. producing results, making quotas, etc. Begin with showing up and consistently demonstrating your capabilities and commitment. Your supervisor or manager is accountable for the results produced by the team. In turn, you are accountable to your supervisor or manager for your productivity. Jack and Suzy Welch express it well in their *Business Week* article, "The importance of Being There" (April 16, 2007) when they say, "Working remotely may be ideal for your lifestyle. But you can't phone in real leadership."

Communicating an understanding of your responsibilities will help you get the training and experience you want/need. Put yourself in your boss's shoes and think about how you can **offer productive suggestions** in line with creating the desired return for the organization.

When you focus your conversation on results and accountability, you will get your supervisor's attention in a positive manner. If, on the other hand, you focus your conversation on how you want to work from home because you like it better, you may come across with an "all about you" attitude. Focus on your team's needs and goals, and help them understand your commitment to the results. Then, share how working from home at 2:00 a.m. and coming in a little later will help you reach the results *they* need.

If there's only one thing you get out of this book, let it be this: "**It's not** *what* **you say, or even** *what* **you ask for — it's** *how* **you say it or** *how* **you ask for it.**"

Many times, young professionals *demand* extra training, time off, or to work when or where they want. When you put the focus on yourself (i.e. "I want this training.") you are likely to come across as self-centered. But when you put the focus on your organization's needs (i.e. "In order to most effectively meet our customer's/organizational needs, it would be helpful for me to get this training.") you are more likely to come across as proactive and a team player. When your career goals are in alignment with your organization's goals, gaining extra training will likely benefit you *and* your organization.

On the other hand, there may be times when you are focused on creating results and find yourself at cross purposes with your co-workers. This happened with a young coaching client, Brad. He came to me extremely frustrated with his co-workers. In order for him to provide the most value to his company, he needed his colleagues to follow an undocumented process he was taught early in his employment. Because his colleagues weren't following the process and cutting corners, Brad was frustrated and annoyed.

I asked him about the process and where it got off track. During his training, he received verbal instruction about the appropriate procedures. Because it was undocumented, I encouraged him to write a guide describing the most effective process and share it with his supervisor. *Doing this took his mind off the problem and focused him on creating a solution.*

Brad was being accountable to what he learned in his training and demonstrating his commitment to the organization with his solution. Begin noticing the many opportunities to add value, tighten up processes and gain visibility all at the same time. When you take action to contributing positive solutions, you *will* be noticed.

Any change worth implementing isn't likely to happen overnight. Assuming that you have found an organization where you can fulfill your career goals, **be patient with the system and committed to your organization.** This long-term commitment will pay off and assist you in eventually getting the position you seek.

Please recognize that no matter what organization you work for, **your reputation will follow you. Make sure you're creating one that you** *want* **to follow you!**

SEASONED PROFESSIONALS

Margaret, a senior manager at a *Fortune* 100 company, was frustrated with some of the young professionals in her department. They would come in late, leave early and wanted to work from home. They wanted more flexibility in their schedules, but Margaret felt the nature of their work made it imperative for them to be in the same building during the workday. She had a high turnover rate and was willing to try something different, but was unsure how to proceed. She requested my assistance in working through this challenge.

I observed two issues. One was an issue of personal control. Seasoned professionals have a tendency to believe that controlling when and how people work is important. Second, the team was not clear about its mission, vision and strategy, making it difficult for the younger professionals to understand how they fit into the larger picture and why their schedules mattered.

Fortunately, Margaret was willing to "let go" of her autocratic leadership style in order for her *entire team* to work on the concern at hand and come up with an acceptable solution.

I brought the team together and facilitated a discussion about their mission/vision, giving everyone an opportunity to contribute ideas. **As the team members became clearer on their contribution** to the mission's success/failure, they were able to create a common strategy and could now understand the importance of being together in person to achieve their goals.

In the interest of creating common ground, Margaret was willing to let go of control and pronouncements (you *should* be here from 9 to 5) and the young professionals on her team were willing to let go of looking only at their own desires (I want to work on my *own* terms).

It's important for senior professionals to take the time to ensure everyone understands the vision/mission and allow for team members to find their own way to a workable strategy, rather than "pulling rank" or attempting to control the situation through inflexibility.

When young professionals have a hand in creating the strategy, they're more likely to be productive team members, accountable for the results they produce.

~ STAYING FOCUSED ~

In *Retiring the Generation Gap, How Employees Young and Old Can Find Common Ground,* Jennifer Deal points out that in actuality, every generation wants the same basic things: to feel valued, to know that what they do matters, opportunities to grow, learn, and advance in their career, and to have a sense of community at work. The biggest difference between generations is the way they express their desires.

Seasoned professionals have been around longer and, as a result, most understand the importance of demonstrating credibility over time and being patient. Many also have a clearer understanding of how to navigate the organizational system. In some cases, they have had more opportunities to try different jobs and, therefore, are often certain about what they like, where their strengths lie and what they want to do.

Today's young professionals, on the other hand, come into organizations with a firm grip on technology, lots of energy and enthusiasm and a fresh set of eyes. Nevertheless, their lack of experience and impatience are both annoying and exceptional at the same time. While many lack clarity regarding their career vision, they are willing to jump in headfirst and learn quickly. As a result of their impatience, young professionals are always looking for a better/faster way of getting work done. Their short cuts may not always be the best, but they are well-intended.

Likewise, seasoned professionals usually have the best of intentions when they argue vehemently to adhere to the way things have always been done. Ultimately, both young and seasoned professionals want to be successful — both as individuals and as part of an organization.

When we understand our differences, it's easier to focus on our commonalties, which, by far, outweigh our differences. When people across generations have personal goals and direction, understand where their organization is going, and receive support along the way, synergy and teamwork are a natural by-product.

There are four basic strategies to create synergy in your organization:

· *Build awareness of personal differences and similarities*

· *Provide opportunities for development and advancement at all levels*

· *Create/promote opportunities for relationship building outside of the work environment*

· *Communicate, Communicate, Communicate*

When we get right down to it, each one of us wants the same basic things. We also appreciate a strong vision/mission and a clear understanding of how we contribute to it. All of us are in a constant state of growth and, as we all know, **the only thing that stays the same is change**. And we each want to insure that change will not leave us behind without a job or career.

Celebrate the fact that we all see the world from different perspectives. These differences *can* (in skill set and perspective) lend great value to the overall success of any team or organization. Likewise, these differences *can* also create barriers to a team's or organization's success.

Anytime you hear team members saying things like: "I want balance," "Nine-to-Five is the way it has always been," "Give me freedom," "Work hard," "Pay your dues," and "Do it my way," you know the focus has veered away from your common vision/mission and differences are not serving your team or organization at that moment.

When the team's or organization's vision/mission is clear and each individual understands how they contribute toward accomplishing that vision/mission, the conversation is set for success. When you add demonstrating appreciation for your employees, compensating them appropriately, giving them opportunities to grow and learn, and allowing their voices to be heard, you have a recipe for success across generations.

REFLECTIONS
CHAPTER SIX

HIGHLIGHTS
CHAPTER SIX

YOUNG PROFESSIONALS

If you desire freedom and flexibility in your
schedule, look for win/win situations.

Put yourself in your boss's shoes and think about
how you can offer productive suggestions in line with
creating the desired return for the company.

"It's not what you say, or even what you ask for —
it's how you say it or how you ask for it."

When you put the focus on your organization's needs
(i.e. "In order to most effectively meet our customer's/organizational
needs, it would be helpful for me to get this training.") you are
more likely to come across as proactive and a team player.

Be patient with the system and stay committed to your organization.

SEASONED PROFESSIONALS

When young professionals have a hand in creating the
strategy (mission), they are more likely to be productive team
members and accountable for the results they produce.

When team members are clear on their contribution to the
mission, and create a common strategy, they will understand the
relevance of the tasks at hand to the goals to be achieved.
As you create this vision/mission and set big goals,
ask volunteers to take on responsibility for the results.

Let go of how they reach their goals. If they reach their targets, keep the customer happy and contribute as a team player, let the rest work itself out.

STAYING FOCUSED

Every generation wants the same basic things:
· To feel valued.
· To know that what they are doing matters.
· Opportunities to grow and learn.
· An opportunity to advance in their career.
· To have a sense of community at work.
· To be successful — both as individuals and as an organization.

The biggest difference between generations is the way they express their desire for the things they want.

When we understand our differences, it's easier to focus on our commonalties.

Recipe for success across generations:
· The team's/organization's vision/mission is clear.
· Each individual understands how they contribute toward accomplishing that vision/mission.
· Appreciation for employees is demonstrated.
· Compensation is appropriate.
· Individuals have opportunities to grow and learn.
· There are vehicles for voices to be heard.

ACCEPTABLE
RISK

SEASONED PROFESSIONALS	COMMON GROUND	YOUNG PROFESSIONALS
5. Adhere to the rules	Creating a common ***strategy*** to reach the vision / Acceptable ***risk***	I can do it faster and better and I have fresh ideas

YOUNG PROFESSIONALS

During a presentation on generational diversity for a sales organization in the Washington, DC area, Rick, a seasoned professional, shared his frustration with the young professionals on his team. "They are more than willing to text message or email a potential client, but for the life of me, I cannot get them to go meet face-to-face with the client."

For the young professionals in question, it was much faster to simply email potential clients or text message existing ones. Apparently, meeting in person took too much time and didn't make sense to them. In fact, many of the young professionals were uncomfortable going to the client site, even if it was for potential new business

While email, instant messaging and text messaging are great tools; they are not a substitute for in-person communication. Some professionals view text messaging as an interruption or annoyance, and emails can easily get lost in the sea of online correspondence. Rick's young professionals didn't understand that **face-time with a client separates you from the pack, builds trust and will undoubtedly lead you to more referrals and sales.**

There have been some valuable changes at Rick's company since I first met him. Rick made an effort to connect his young professionals with seasoned professionals by sending them out together to meet with clients. As a result, I saw a shift among Rick's young professionals as they learned the importance of face-to-face communication. As the year progressed, these workers needed less guidance and were learning to establish relationships on their own. Furthermore, they created their own unique ways of interacting in person and aren't intimidated by people with whom they need to build relationships. By pushing through something that seemed uncomfortable at first, these young professionals experienced personal growth and built their confidence to higher levels. Rick continues to provide mentors and demonstrate why connecting in person is so important.

Sometimes the way it has always been done *is* the best way. Be patient with both yourself and your employer. **Take the time to learn proven methods** and the reasons for them. Once you have explored these systems, you may realize the benefits of existing protocols and subsequently, use your ingenuity to enhance them. If you approach your supervisor with the big picture in mind and show them how your ideas will benefit the organization, they'll be much more likely to listen.

Ultimately, your organization needs to remain focused on the bottom line. Without a strong bottom line, no one in your organization has a job!

Even if your company doesn't have a mentoring program, young professionals can take initiative and request "shadow" opportunities with seasoned professionals in order to learn a skill from someone who has hands-on experience.

SEASONED PROFESSIONALS

While speaking to a large shipping company, I had a humorous conversation with Judy, a Generation Xer who works in the technology department. Judy was in charge of updating and upgrading their system's tracking process with the intention of making it more efficient.

Judy was working on the system used to count the number of trips made by a delivery person. The system being used was as old as the company (over 100 years old!) and clearly needed updating. As Judy began putting new processes in place, the seasoned staff began protesting the changes. Most of them had been with the company for a long time and were used to their routine. They, like many of us, didn't like the idea of change and were resistant.

Curious, I asked Judy how she approached the seasoned professionals who were clearly reluctant to change. She looked at me with a smile and said, "Well, I realized they may not know why this system needed updating or what it may do for the company's success. So, I explained to them the current system was first implemented back when the company used horses and carriages for shipping. After many of them laughed, they understood the need for a new system and simply wanted to know how they would be trained on it."

Are you using a system that is no longer necessary or effective? Inside most large organizations I have assisted, I hear the words "red tape" constantly. Essentially, employees are saying that their organization's systems are not the most effective or efficient. As organizations grow, the natural reflex of most leaders is to create systems for everything. While some systems or processes are necessary, many cause more delay in productivity than they're worth.

The trick is finding the balance, which has everything to do with listening to your employees' frustrations and finding a way to help them be their most productive. Sometimes it makes sense to look at what systems are in use, why they were implemented and then consider current needs. **Work with your team to create new systems that make the most sense for your organization today.** Because they're not "attached" to the current system, younger employees may have unique ideas that will actually make things run more smoothly. Once those ideas are approved, give them the responsibility to implement their ideas. When this is done consistently, as a matter of course, morale increases and employees are more productive.

Some companies even offer employee suggestion programs that encourage workers to provide ideas to increase efficiency and productivity. If an idea is accepted and implemented, the employee is justly rewarded. **It takes a brave and committed leader** to create necessary change and remove unnecessary processes that are preventing staff members from doing their jobs efficiently.

REFLECTIONS
CHAPTER SEVEN

HIGHLIGHTS
CHAPTER SEVEN

YOUNG PROFESSIONALS

Face time with a client and/or professional in the position
to promote you will separate you from the pack, build trust and
will likely lead you to more referrals, sales and promotions.

Take the time to learn proven methods and the reasons
for them. Once you have explored these systems,
you may realize the benefits of existing protocols and
subsequently use your ingenuity to enhance them.

Focus on creating solutions rather
than complaining about the problem.

SEASONED PROFESSIONALS

Take time to listen to young professionals' suggestions.
When appropriately directed, their confusion and frustration
can lead to solutions that will benefit everyone.

Look at the bigger picture and work with your team to create new
systems that make the most sense for your organization today.

Younger employees may have unique ideas
that will actually make things run more smoothly.
Once those ideas are approved, give employees
the responsibility to implement their ideas.
It takes a brave and committed leader to create necessary
change and remove unnecessary red tape that's preventing
staff members from doing their jobs efficiently.

Employee Suggestion Programs offer a structured
opportunity for staff members to suggest ideas that will
increase efficiency and productivity. If an idea is accepted
and implemented, the employee is justly rewarded.

CREATE A SENSE OF COMMUNITY

According to a 2006 research study by SelectMind, a corporate social network solutions provider, "Today's youngest workers are bringing a new sense of importance to workplace relationships. More than three-quarters (77%) of workers age 20-29 believe that the social aspects of work are very important to their overall sense of workplace satisfaction, compared with 67% of their older colleagues."

The study further states, "When transitioning into a new job, Gen Yers rank 'cementing relationships with colleagues and supervisors' (41%) as their number one challenge, ahead of learning the new job responsibilities (27%) and adapting to a new company culture (33%). For many of these young workers, relationships function as an information 'search engine,' providing them with information that is pre-qualified and, therefore, credible." This was true for Veronica at ABC Company, as was discussed in Chapter Four.

Quoted in the November 2006 issue of *T+D* (a magazine of the American Society for Training & Development), research by The Corporate Leadership Council suggests that new employees decide within the first 30 days whether they feel welcome in the organization.

Further emphasizing the need for networking programs, SelectMind's study also concluded that, "Nearly half (46%) of these Gen Yers also rate the availability of support/networking programs for employees with common interests (new mothers, pre-retirees, new mid-career hires and recent graduates) as a very important factor in their decision to join and/or remain with an employer, compared with 36% of their peers."

Creating community seems like such a simple idea with a great outcome, yet few organizations make it a priority. When I think of organizations that do a great job creating a community among professionals, two companies come to mind. The first one, a law firm in Maryland, does an outstanding job creating community among all levels within the firm. In order to keep people around during lunch and help them get to know each other, the firm buys lunch for everyone from a local restaurant every day.

No one is forced to eat at the firm every day, but most days co-workers do end up eating together at the office, chatting over lunch. Because they **spend less time out of the office** going for lunch, they're able to get more done and have time to connect with each other. In addition to providing lunch daily, the firm throws a few parties throughout the year, which brings family members into the mix as well. Its retention rate is extremely high and most employees work well together. The company has really done a great job!

> *"You can discover more about a person in an hour of play than in a year of conversation."*
>
> PLATO

The second company, a video game company in Virginia, brings lunch in periodically and occasionally rents out an entire movie theater or bowling alley in the middle of the day, encouraging employees at all levels to attend with their family members. The company also throws a big party during the holidays and invite friends and family. At the beginning of every summer it rents an outdoor space and throws a barbeque with plenty of special activities for employees and their families.

Both companies understand the importance of creating community among their employees. It's common to see the **executives from both companies participate in most of the events.** Their participation adds to their credibility as leaders and to the cohesiveness of the company.

Creating opportunities for people to get to know each other where title, project or experience level doesn't matter, makes for even greater working relationships. It's this simple: **People who know and like each other are far more likely to work well together.**

When individual leaders begin conducting small outings with their team, they create an even stronger bond among team members. Good leaders ask staff members for ideas. Below are some possible activities to get you started:

- *Roller Skating/Ice Skating*

- *Bowling*

- *Go out for lunch/ordering in*

- *Barbeque*

- *Beach Day*

- *Softball*

- *Creative, friendly competition in teams (perhaps to make something that will be donated to a children's hospital or orphanage)*

- *Treasure or Scavenger Hunt in teams*

- *Hiking*

- *Chili Cook-off*

- *Community service — painting an elderly person's house, fixing up a playground, visiting folks in a nursing home or children in the hospital, etc.*

Young professionals are interested in work/life balance, so doing such activities during working hours will be well received. Rewarding your team through outside activities is a wonderful way to keep them charged up.

If you're concerned about the amount of time it takes to create and attend such activities, let me remind you how **much more will be accomplished as a result of building strong relationships and enhancing cohesiveness between employees.** Making these activities a priority sends a powerful message to your employees. Your presence also ensures that employees from all levels of your organization feel important.

This reminds me of a story about a large financial services company that held what was announced as an exciting teambuilding weekend. The only problem: Executives stayed at a more expensive hotel and didn't participate in any of the activities, except meals!

This is definitely NOT the way to build morale and team spirit. Leader participation in community building events is critical. It's just as important for leaders and teams to get to know each other informally as it is for team members to get to know each other. In other words, providing opportunities for employees to build relationships, regardless of level, is important to the success of each employee and, in turn, the entire organization.

REFLECTIONS
CHAPTER EIGHT

HIGHLIGHTS
CHAPTER EIGHT

More than three-quarters (77 percent) of workers age
20-29 believe the social aspects of work are very important
to their overall sense of workplace satisfaction.

Gen Yers rank "cementing relationships with colleagues
and supervisors" as their number one challenge (41 percent),
ahead of learning the new job responsibilities (27 percent)
and adapting to a new company culture (33 percent).

Creating an opportunity for people to get to know one
another, without concern for titles, experience level
or projects, makes for better working relationships.

People who know and like each other are
far more likely to work well together.

Executive participation in social events
adds to their credibility as leaders
and builds cohesiveness within the company.

Individual managers can step out and begin
conducting small outings with their teams to create
an even stronger bond among team members.

LEADING ACROSS GENERATIONS

Whether you're a young or seasoned professional, leading across generations requires an understanding of each generation, what makes it tick, and the best ways to motivate and support its members in their unique development. When implementing strategies to boost productivity and employee retention, it's most important to **create and encourage personal connections, demonstrate an interest in employee success, provide feedback and show appreciation frequently.**

During a coaching session with Brad, a senior executive at a *Fortune* 5 company, he said, in an exasperated voice, "The concepts we talk about during our coaching sessions are so simple. I know and understand them. Somewhere along the way, I just forgot their importance. Of course, I need to begin doing them again."

While the ideas I share throughout this book are simple in nature, they require consistent attention. We all need reminders to get back to the basic, simple things that work. Life gets complicated and stressful, and we forget that our best results often come from consistently returning to what matters most — the human side of the business and the focus on the vision and mission. At the same time, young professionals may be unfamiliar with the elements listed above to bring about necessary changes. Sometimes, we are so caught up in the issues of the day that we really don't know where to start.

As a leader, a great place to begin with your employees is to **ask them for feedback** on your leadership style — a 360 degree assessment. The only way to get honest feedback is to ensure your employees there will be no backlash. Assure them that their ideas and suggestions will help you grow as a leader, which will benefit everyone in the long run. While it's usually best to have such an assessment conducted by a professional from outside your organization, it is possible for you to begin the process on your own. Mind you, this takes a great deal of courage. *And* it's well worth it! By facing the truth and making modifications, leaders can propel themselves and their teams to new heights.

> *"Most great people have attained their greatest success just one step beyond their greatest failure."*
>
> NAPOLEON HILL
> *Author,* Think and Grow Rich

Several months ago, I requested that Jack, a coaching client, seek feedback on his leadership style. He left my office excited to complete this exercise and ready to make some adjustments. Two weeks later, he returned — without having begun the process. Jack was failing to reach his sales quota for three consecutive years and needed to make some modifications quickly. His job was on the line!

He wanted everything to simply be "smoothed over" and "get back to normal," without first learning what changes needed to be made. At the time, he couldn't admit that he was failing. He wanted to keep pretending that everything was OK and hope that somehow things would change.

In order to make authentic, long-lasting change, you MUST face what's real. You must start where you are and build from there.

Eventually, Jack did take the huge step of admitting his difficulties to his team and asking for their support in reaching the team's goals. He shared his need to grow as a leader and began making small adjustments immediately. As his team members made suggestions, he gave each of them the responsibility for bringing their ideas to fruition.

As a direct result of Jack getting involved with his people, being honest with them and working together on their mission, the team surpassed its quota for the first time in three years! It was a victory for Jack *and* for his team. The reality is that **we *all* have room to grow**. Just like life, **leadership is a process**.

Successfully demonstrating that process is Masoud, a 25-year-old commercial executive in charge of business development for a community bank. He's clearly quite motivated and willing to do what's necessary to succeed — both for his own career and for the bank. He realizes the importance of developing the people he works with in order to achieve success. But Masoud was unsure about how to motivate seasoned employees who were feeling a little disenchanted or unmotivated. He asked for ideas to inspire his seasoned staff.

After working diligently on this issue, he had these points to share about leading across generations:

· *First off, you must respect the people on your team.*

· *Next, motivation drives motivation. My co-workers feed off my exuberance and do things they never thought they could.*

· *Young professionals feel that they are capable of taking on responsibility now. They want to cut right to it. Their mentality and actions scream, "Give me a shot and let me prove I can handle anything you throw at me." To seasoned professionals (Baby Boomers), that is completely backwards. They are accustomed to "earning their stripes" before getting the fancy title or largest account, corner office, etc. If you receive a shot over someone older, remember you now have to prove you can do it and hold your own. When you give it your best, seasoned professionals will look at you and think, "He/She does deserve to be here, let's help him/her." Don't forget, you probably got the shot from a Baby Boomer who saw your glimmering potential.*

Masoud emphasizes that learning the strengths and weaknesses of your team is extremely important:

- *Help them where they're weak without directly pointing it out. If, for example, you're lucky enough for a co-worker (especially a Boomer) to ask you to proofread a document and writing is not one of that person's strong points, don't just point out errors with red marks, ask "Do you mind if I make some changes?" This shows that you're respectful of their knowledge and courteous of their feelings. You can never take advantage of a person's weakness or throw it in their face, directly or indirectly.*

- *Ask seasoned professionals (Boomers) for their assistance in areas where you are challenged and they are strong. They have a great deal of knowledge and love to share. This shows them you are willing to acknowledge your own shortcomings, so, embrace their wealth. It may also open them up to learning from you, too.*

- *Bask in the glory with your team rather than keeping it all for yourself. This is very motivating!*

Here is more key information to assist leaders in addressing this challenge:

AWARENESS

While it's easy to get caught up in our own world, our own experiences, and assume we understand the experiences of others, it's important to realize that every generation grew up with different experiences and seminal events shaping the way they see the world. These experiences dramatically affect behaviors, thought patterns and attitudes.

For example, young professionals are, by and large, hugely optimistic, constantly wanting to grow and learn and looking to move ahead as quickly as possible. In contrast, seasoned professionals, for the most part, came into the workforce with fewer career choices and simply focused on whatever position they were able to obtain. Their message was "work hard to get ahead."

Young professionals grew up with instant gratification, "faster = better" mentality. They received an award for simply playing on the team. Seasoned professionals grew up with a "pay your dues" mentality, a belief in adherence to rules and a process for everything. Now, they find themselves being managed by "little whippersnappers" who have, what they *believe* to be a disrespectful attitude and who think they "know everything." Consider this for a minute, young professionals — wouldn't you find that annoying too?

Few young professionals realize that while women worked outside the home during World War II, doing "men's jobs," when the war was over, the men took

> "Do not judge your neighbor until you walk two moons in his moccasins."
>
> CHEYENNE PROVERB

their jobs back and the women returned home. It was Baby Boomers who truly set the stage for women in the workforce on a full-time basis, not just as temporary substitutes for absent men. As such, many never thought about what they would like to do or the type of job they might thrive in most. They took what was available, "appropriate for their gender," and worked hard.

Now, young professionals are entering the workforce with enthusiasm, an abundance of choices, and little understanding of previous generations' experience. **Taking the time to learn about another's experience will give you the tools to work effectively with people of different generations.**

UNDERSTANDING

With a clear understanding and openness to stylistic differences between the generations, you can learn to "speak their language" and identify ways to motivate your multi-generational team. **While young professionals might be motivated by an opportunity to take on a big project early in their careers, seasoned professionals may be motivated by an opportunity to mentor or share their experiences with your team.**

To gain a richer understanding of the people working with/for you, consider asking questions about their early experiences in the workforce. You might ask about their future aspirations. If they don't have career plans, you can help them determine their strengths and career path — thereby giving them something to expand into.

WHEN A LEADER TAKES AN INTEREST ...

I was giving a speech on generational diversity to 150 executive women. In the middle of a passionate moment about the importance of mentoring, a woman named Joan raised her hand to share a poignant story.

She spoke of an older gentleman, Fred, who had worked in the proposal-writing department of the same company for more than 20 years — Joan had worked there for almost 10 years. While Fred always showed up on time, did a good job and never really caused any problems, he rarely had a smile on his face and didn't seem to enjoy coming to work. About two years prior to this conference, the company had been acquired and a new management team had taken over.

As a result, Fred began reporting to a new manager. **She took an active interest in her employees**, asked a lot of questions, and learned about everyone's passions and interests, including Fred's.

While Fred had been writing proposals for more than 18 years and knew how to do it, he was never really passionate about the work. He didn't think it was possible to do what he really enjoyed and didn't even know what that might be!

Over time, the new manager helped Fred explore his interests. In less than two years, she helped him discover that fulfilling his passion required a move into the business development department. Since his move, Joan has never seen Fred so visibly happy — "He actually seems excited to be at work — it's not just a job anymore."

Fred spent 20 years working in a position where he performed his job well, but not really enjoying it. Thankfully, a caring manager came into his life, encouraged him to think through his interests and helped him move into a more satisfying position. Imagine how different the first 20 years could have been if Fred had taken the time to learn about his interests, consider his options and apply for positions that fit his passion. While many sales professionals develop these kinds of relationships with their customers, few leaders take the time to do so with their employees. Imagine the difference it will make in their output when you do!

To best gain an understanding of your team members, ask questions and then **truly listen** to their response. Most people never really get to be heard — you will stand out for them when you give them this gift. You will also acquire valuable information on what motivates them. By the way, this is the same advice I give seasoned professionals on how to inspire young professionals and create loyalty! *You* be the change you wish to see, regardless of the generation you are leading.

EMBRACE DIFFERENCES

Most people have a natural tendency to want to surround themselves with people who are just like them. When hiring, they look for people who are similar to them and, therefore, easy to lead. While there certainly is value in searching for specific attitudes and skill sets, there's an added benefit of different perspectives and strengths that automatically comes with including different age groups.

When you let go of wanting your employees to be a certain way, and you become aware of their strengths and primary motivators, the entire team — and organization — benefits. Thank goodness we're not all the same or motivated in the same ways, or life would be very boring and much too competitive! **The sooner we embrace our differences, the sooner we can use those differences to achieve more, together.**

If you have an older employee pushing you to understand his or her rationale for using a particular method, take the time to listen — you just might see something you didn't previously notice. When you listen to and support people of older generations, you create an opportunity for shared learning, community and cohesiveness.

We all want to feel a sense of connection — a sense that we're part of something larger than our-

> *"People in organizations are primarily looking for meaning in their work. But not many leaders act as though they believe that's what really motivates people. They think money motivates people. At the end of the day, people want to know they've done something meaningful."*
>
> BILL GEORGE

> *"The most basic and powerful way to connect to another person is to listen. Just listen. Perhaps the most important thing we ever give each other is our attention."*
>
> RACHEL NAOMI REMEN

selves. *Anyone*, regardless of age or position, can help create that by listening, sharing and being open to different ways of seeing.

Again, this is the same thing I encourage seasoned professionals to do. Remember, **we're creating a bridge and neither side of the bridge is "right" or "wrong," — the viewpoint is simply different**. Regardless of generation, focusing on what's most important (i.e., developing your people, growing your business, and achieving your mission) will serve you and your organization well!

GET CREATIVE

Just as young professionals need to explore career passions and possibilities, so do seasoned professionals. My first coaching session with Mary, a seasoned professional with a *Fortune* 5 company, was truly memorable. She had spent the past 25 years working her way into an executive position. As we began our first session, she said, "I have absolutely no idea what I want to do with my career — I've always just taken whatever came my way. Now I'm ready for something different, but I don't know what."

Realizing the abundance of options in front of her now, she wanted to begin exploring. When I first asked her to come up with a list of tasks/activities she enjoyed or might like to try, she could only think about her current position. While this was a great place to start, I encouraged her to think beyond what she had already experienced.

At first she looked at me blankly — she had no idea what else was available. However, with a willingness to explore and learn more about possible career avenues, Mary slowly began reaching out to her colleagues to make connections and conduct informational interviews (See Chapter Thirteen to learn more about informational interviews). While this was a bit of a stretch outside of her comfort zone, she ventured forth. These interviews opened her eyes to new possibilities and she began getting excited about what might be next for her career.

In reality, many seasoned professionals are in a position similar to Mary's. They have worked hard their whole lives, many achieving great career success, but feel stuck, unmotivated and unsure of their future. Most people never take the time to get to know themselves or consider what they really want in a job or career. With no real understanding of what they might like to do differently, they simply continue to take whatever comes their way.

Regardless of age, these are people who need great leadership. They need someone to ask important questions about their likes/dislikes so they can express their passion through work, rather than just dragging themselves through each day, not being as productive as they could be.

Some are lucky enough to find a profession that matches their unique talents and natural interests, but a greater number end up in positions they dislike and frustration results. A 2004 Gallup pole indicated that more than 70 percent of employees are "disengaged clock watchers." **You're far more likely to be "engaged" if you know what you like, have a plan for the future and are doing what you are good at and enjoy.**

If you never take time to get to know yourself, your likes/dislikes, the type of position you want and why you want it, it will be difficult for you to find job satisfaction. If you don't know where you're going, it's hard to map out a route to get there.

Imagine, for a moment, a life where everyone took the time to explore their passions and find a job where they could express that passion. Customers would almost always have a great experience! And instead of succumbing to a sense of drudgery about going to work, people would more likely feel excited about their jobs and look ahead to a bright future. As a result of really enjoying their work, they would be happier and healthier, both mentally and physically. Instead of feeling that their work controls them, they would feel empowered in a profession that best suits their interests.

GET INTO ACTION

For young professionals, with fresh set of eyes, techno-savvy minds and great enthusiasm, there is vast opportunity in reverse mentorship. Find creative ways to recognize the seasoned generation's strengths and the enormity of their experience. Find opportunities for their voices to be heard and ways for them to add value by sharing their knowledge and skills. Providing a platform for them to share and contribute to the team will boost morale among all generations. One way to create this platform within your team is to select a time, perhaps once or twice a month, for team members to make a presentation to the group. Let them choose the topic. This will allow everyone on your team to contribute.

Another great way to motivate your team across generations is to meet with each member individually and **ask what motivates them**. If they're clearly stuck in their career, **help them begin exploring new possibilities**. This process is similar to what I recommend young professionals do for themselves. The only difference is that seasoned professionals have more experience and perhaps a better understanding of what works for them.

The concept of conducting informational interviews may be a bit outside some workers' comfort zone. If that is the case, you might **help them find individuals whose jobs they consider interesting** and recommend they go to coffee or lunch to learn more. In essence, you're helping them develop their network and explore other possibilities for leveraging their strengths.

If employees aren't open to this sort of exploration process, determine what they are open to. They may have ideas about training they would like to receive or groups they have an interest in joining. **When you are truly committed to people's success, they will recognize it.** Ultimately you and your organization will also benefit greatly as a result of their renewed interest in their own success. As they succeed, you and your organization will also succeed.

Put simply, leading across generations requires:

· *Enlightened leadership*

· *A clear vision/mission*

· *Providing opportunities to grow and learn*

· *Systems for advancement at all levels*

· *An open door policy*

· *Rotational internship programs*

· *Mentorship programs*

Instead of labeling others "wrong" or "right" for the way they act or speak, avoid taking it personally. Take action instead. Recognize the magnitude of this *huge* opportunity for exploration and learning among the most diverse generations in history! When leaders **at all levels** challenge their own assumptions and ideas about the way work "should" be done and focus on both their organization's mission and their employees' strengths and goals, the resulting synergy will lead to organizational and employee success.

"For me, leadership begins with an honest self-assessment, understanding your strengths and weaknesses, and being able to build a leadership style that is consistent with who you are. After you have established who you are as a leader, establish a vision for your team, clearly articulate your standards and expectations, and inspect what you expect. Lastly, celebrate the big achievements, recognize the little things and always have a kind word for the people that you work with!"

XAVIER WILLIAMS, V.P.

REFLECTIONS
CHAPTER NINE

HIGHLIGHTS

CHAPTER NINE

We are creating a bridge and neither side is "right"
or "wrong." They simply have different perspectives.

Your staff will feed off your motivation.

Seasoned professionals are accustomed to
earning stripes after putting in the time.

Young professionals want to "get right to it"
and earn their stripes as they go along.

To be successful across generations:
· Create a personal connection.
· Demonstrate an interest in your team's success.
· Provide feedback from which team members can grow.
· Show appreciation regularly.

Ask seasoned professionals for help in areas
where you are weak and they are strong. Share the
glory you receive for your resulting success.

Ask your team for feedback on your leadership.

In order to make authentic, long-lasting change,
you MUST face what's real so you can start
where you are and build from there.

(CONTINUED)

Build Awareness: Taking the time to learn about another's experience will give you the tools to work effectively with people of different generations.

Develop Understanding: To best gain an understanding of your team members, ask questions and then truly listen to their response.

Embrace Differences: The sooner we can embrace our differences, the sooner we can use those differences to achieve more.

Get Creative: Find creative ways to utilize the skills, experience, knowledge and ability of the seasoned professionals whom you manage.

Take Action: Recognize the strengths of each generation, and the contribution they can make.

When you are truly committed to an individual's success, they will recognize it.

THE BENEFIT OF ROTATIONAL INTERNSHIP PROGRAMS

Many young professionals have never really considered what they like, why they like it or what they may want to do next. Add to that an abundance of options and incredible pressure to "be successful" right away, and you have a group of people wanting to be in the corner office leading people, with no clear understanding of why they want this or how to get there.

Rotational internship programs allow young professionals an opportunity to explore their interests and gain experience across your organization. Add a well-structured mentorship program to a well-structured rotational internship program and you have just created an excellent way to cultivate leaders from within your organization.

Providing an opportunity for young professionals to gain experience across your organization allows both the prospective employee and employer to gain a feel for where the intern fits best with no long-term commitments on either side. Interns have the opportunity to gain skills and experience while building a reputation for themselves. The organization and its seasoned professionals have the opportunity to "test drive" young professionals and determine what position, if any, will best suit their talents.

A recent Gallup study demonstrated more than 70 percent of U.S. workers admit that they see their jobs as merely a means to pick up a paycheck. Imagine how effective your organization would be if the majority of your employees were engaged. Imagine what engaged employees could produce if you directed effort toward developing their skills and placing them in a position that best suits their goals and abilities.

According to the Gallup study, your return on investment would be in the billions, depending on the size of your organization. Yet according to a 2003 study by research and consulting firm Best Practices, LLC, when organizations go through budget reductions, they usually cut from human resources first. Considering the importance of employee satisfaction to your bottom line, this is the worst decision an organization can make.

> *"The opposite of trusting in the unexpected is trying to control the uncontrollable — clearly an impossible task."*
>
> ANGELES ARRIEN

In today's fast paced, demanding world, I recognize the leadership and organizational challenge of finding time and resources to support young professionals in this way. Nevertheless, taking time and resources to create a well-developed mentor and internship program will, without question, pay off in the long run!

Here are some important tips for creating rotational internship programs:

TIP ONE: PROVIDE OPPORTUNITIES EARLY AND OFTEN

Today's young professionals are most interested in practical experiences from which they can gain hands-on exposure/experience quickly. I often hear leaders express reluctance about giving young professionals opportunities too early. Comments range from: "They haven't proven themselves yet." to "They need to pay their dues first." Without question, the idea of providing big opportunities early on is radically different from the way things were done in the past.

Providing young workers with opportunities that may seem outside their experience level will demonstrate your trust and confidence in them while giving them an opportunity to demonstrate their abilities. (Recall the intern story in Chapter Four.) Recognize, of course, that they may make mistakes and require more guidance. Fortunately, when you take time to coach and mentor young employees early in the process, you won't need to spend as much time with them going forward. As a result, your time will be freed up to do other things and young professionals get the experiences and exposure they desire.

I will never forget the excitement in the voice of a young medical student who was interning at a clinic: "I thought all I was going to be allowed to do was answer the phone, file and check patients in. They are actually bringing me in to assist them in treating patients. I'm getting real-world experience. I love it here!" Do you think this young man would consider taking a job at this clinic after graduating? He did!

The reality is, there are phones to be answered and papers to be filed — every organization has many needs. Providing opportunities early on doesn't mean losing support with the smaller (less visible) tasks. Rather, **including big opportunities early, in conjunction with other necessary tasks, provides a great balance**. Young professionals need to learn the less visible, tedious parts of the business as well; creating balance is key.

Remember: If your goal is to empower young professionals and create loyalty, I encourage you to stay focused on that goal. Providing opportunities early, and coaching/mentoring immediately are important steps in the direction of employee retention and loyalty, which I encourage you to take.

TIP TWO: CREATE COMMUNITY AMONG INTERNS

I was coaching an executive at a large hotel chain a few years ago. I remember her describing the way some young professionals behaved while at work. A bit annoyed, she explained that they would all come to work at the same time, take breaks at the same time, go to lunch at the same time and leave at the same time. She saw this activity as immature and wondered why they weren't using that time to develop relationships with seasoned employees and get ahead on work. "They all want to get ahead quickly and none of them are willing to put in extra energy to develop important relationships. Don't they understand they have to prove themselves?"

No, they don't! They need a support structure and guidance. They are comfortable with each other and don't realize how important it is to reach out and engage with other co-workers and managers. This is why mentoring programs and guided internship programs are so important.

Let's face it, **when we feel connected and part of a team, we're more likely to *want* to stay engaged.** Young professionals, particularly those just out of college, may not naturally know how to create a network — or even know they need one — but they do want to feel as though they are part of a team. Likewise, spending time with similarly-minded people is natural during an adjustment period.

Creating community for interns develops a sense of belonging. When they were in school, there were many groups to belong to; by simply being in college, they were part of a group and helped to create community. Developing relationships when entering the workforce is challenging for most young professionals.

Here are two effective, yet simple, ways to create community among interns (and young professionals):

· *Offer a monthly casual outing paid for by the company (i.e. bowling, a hike, dinner, lunch); something that allows people to interact with one another and get to know each other. Going to the movies is fun, but it doesn't provide an appropriate environment for talking and getting to other people.*

· *Such outings are a great way to create community among all ages and professional levels. And think about the message it sends when executives attend these gatherings: "All employees are valuable," "The executives are 'real' people too," "The executives care about people from all levels." It's never so much what you say, as what you do, that matters most.*

· *Start a young professionals networking group that meets monthly to discuss challenges and share ideas. If possible, provide a small budget for speakers or other training that employees may find valuable. This will provide them with an opportunity to learn from each other and strategize together.*

(For more on creating community, see Chapter Eight.)

TIP THREE: PROVIDE A MENTOR

Many seasoned professionals feel young professionals don't want to be mentored because, "They think they already know everything." While their behavior or conversation may lead you to believe they don't want mentorship, realize they don't always know how they are coming across. In addition, many are afraid to come across as "unknowing" — they think that they are somehow immediately supposed to know how things work. Stop for a moment and remember what it was like for you when you first entered the workforce. It's very likely you will recall some of the same frustrations.

TIP FOUR: REQUEST FEEDBACK — WHAT'S WORKING/WHAT'S NOT

The worst thing a company or a leader can do is to assume they're acquainted with all the problems — even if they have heard "all the rumors." Corporate structure is similar in nature to the human body: The location of the pain is not necessarily the location of the actual problem. Many times the true problem has nothing to do with the surfacing pain.

Consider for a moment that **your employees are at least as valuable as your customers.** Without employees, there would be no one to serve your customers. Further, the way employees are treated will affect their attitude and morale, which in turn, affects the way they treat your customers. This inevitably influences your customers' decisions. In short, retaining your employees requires as much consideration as retaining your customers.

I frequently get phone calls from leaders who say, "Young professionals keep making huge demands, asking for things that make no sense for our business." These demands range from flex time, to faster upward mobility, to visibility, just to name a few. What's underneath these requests is usually **a need to feel a sense of accomplishment and forward movement.** Additionally, many employees want to know that what they do matters — i.e. they want to feel valuable. Truly, all people want to feel valuable!

Remember, these young professionals grew up seeing what employee loyalty did and didn't do for their parents. **They understand the importance of continuing their education and improving their abilities and experiences.** If they don't, they know they could get left behind.

Additionally, they grew up in an instant gratification world — they're looking for instant gratification in their career as well. This isn't "right" or "wrong" — it just is! When they aren't focused on their development and experience level, for many, fear sets in and they get impatient. If you're saying, "That's just wrong and they clearly need to get it," you're missing the point.

The quicker you can adjust without judgment, the faster your team/organization will move ahead. Young professionals' need for instant gratification and constant feedback can easily be addressed in your organization by **providing opportunities and creating additional levels.**

There are many ways to show appreciation. **Bring the team together and get creative.** Ask for suggestions. It takes little time, costs little and will make a big impact toward retention in your organization.

Imagine the message it would send if organizational executives called a meeting with all young professionals to **ask what's working well, what can be done better** and what changes can be made immediately. Of course, **listening with an open mind is the key to hearing the full truth and gaining young professionals' loyalty.**

> *"Treat people as if they are what they ought to be, and you help them become what they are capable of being."*
> GOETHE

Further, consider the message you send when the organization begins implementing employee ideas immediately. If their ideas require time and effort, ask young professionals to take on the responsibility for ensuring success. **Let them volunteer to participate in the implementation of their great ideas.** Having *them* take action will take the work off your desk and show them first-hand their value to your organization.

TIP FIVE: USE A MINIMUM OF FOUR ROTATIONS — TWO YEARS — PROVIDE OPTIONS

A two-year commitment, offering a minimum of four rotations, will help young professionals stay focused while allowing your organization a time period from which to gain clarity around company/employee fit. Over the course of two years, a young professional can gain good experience, testing out their likes/dislikes across four areas and be prepared to select the best fit for their talents and desires. They will gain knowledge and experience across the organization, while building relationships and learning about different areas of the organization. This is a win/win for both company and employee. When employees are in jobs they are naturally good at and like, they're more apt to work harder.

This experience will greatly benefit the long-term success of both the organization and the young professionals. **As future leaders, they will have a foundation of understanding in at least four separate areas and will have built relationships along the way.**

TIP SIX: CREATE A WELL-STRUCTURED PROCESS

I've heard many seasoned professionals say of young professionals, "If they would just stay focused on doing a good job and be patient, they'll get ahead. That's what I did." But when I look at their organization's statistics, almost without fail, their retention rates are very low.

When young professionals don't have to concern themselves with how the process will unfold, they can stay focused on the tasks at hand. Consider this example: You decide you want to put a new swimming pool in your backyard. So, you do a quick Google search and find several local pool installation companies. You call two companies and ask them to come do an estimate. The sales representative from the first company shows up, looks around your house, writes down some variables, comes up with an estimate and tells you how much it will cost.

The sales representative from the second company shows up, asks you a series of questions to ensure he knows exactly what you want, walks around your home to take note of all the variables, then sits down with you to make sure he understands your desires completely.

> *"It is what we do easily and what we like to do that we do well."*
> **ORISON SWETT MARDEN**
> *Motivational author*

From there, the sales representative echoes back the concerns he heard you express, asks if there are more and walks you through exactly what you can expect if you choose his company. In fact, to make it even easier for you, he provides a one-page brochure that clearly explains the process, as well as the timeframe for completion. Before his sales rep leaves, he provides you with a couple of references so you can hear what others have to say about his company's work and even provides an address where you can actually view past projects.

Which company would you choose to install your new pool? Company two, of course! The last thing you want is to have to think through all the details of putting in a swimming pool. That is, after all, why you're hiring a professional!

So, how does this relate to your employees? Very simply, create a process for new hires and interns that takes the guesswork out of what is required to move forward in the organization. **When they see a clear path for success and know how to navigate it, they're far more likely to want to stay.** It's when they don't know how to navigate your system that they begin looking for opportunities elsewhere.

If your intention is to retain talent, consider the small adjustments you can make to help young professionals experience success. Use the swimming pool sales analogy for your organization. **What adjustments can you make to create an environment where your employees of all ages can thrive?** Begin asking! Then take action to create solid systems for retaining talent.

TIP SEVEN: FINDING INTERNS IS EASY — WITH THE RIGHT PROCESS

Before searching for interns, you need to be clear on what qualities, skills and personality traits you prefer and how you will interview candidates. Get the process down first, then put the word out.

There are two great ways to find good interns. **The first, and best, is to allow current employees/interns to help you.** Ask your best employees to help you find more great people just like them. What a splendid compliment! Add a financial incentive for recruiting and you have just created another excellent way to reward your staff. Young professionals are such outstanding electronic communicators that they can get the word out in very little time. When the organization does a great job taking care of its people, the recruiting process is much easier. If you want to attract great people, treat your people well and they will attract more just like them.

Another way to attract quality interns is to **build relationships with**

students and professors at nearby colleges and universities. As with all your relationships (customers, employees, recruiting), treat these professors like the volunteers they are, and watch what they do for you. Go the extra mile to help them feel appreciated and valued and they will refer their best students to you. People help people they like and people generally like those who treat them well. It's that simple!

You can carry this idea one step further: A great leader once told me, "Treat everyone as if they are a volunteer and just see what happens." I understand it may be difficult to think of paid employees as volunteers. But when you implement this philosophy, you may find that they end up working harder and producing in ways you would never have imagined!

~ AN AWARD-WINNING INTERNSHIP PROGRAM ~

Post Properties, a Real Estate Investment Trust (REIT), develops and manages residential properties in nine markets across the United States. Over the past three years, its leaders have developed a solid, HR Excellence award-winning internship program, for which they recruit rising college seniors in order to teach them about the leasing side of the business. Interns come in direct contact with a third of Post's organization, from the CEO on down, as well as a significant number of residents and future customers. The Post internship is a real life on-the-job experience.

Some students are interested in becoming residential property managers; others are finance or marketing majors.

Before this program was developed, Post only offered an internship on the landscaping side. Then the company shifted its expectations to hiring all college graduates for management training, starting with leasing specialists.

Program leaders researched local universities' objectives for internship programs, which helped add more structure and a sense of direction and purpose — for both Post and its interns. Interns are recruited from 23 universities in the nine markets served by Post Properties. In 2007 the program included 15 interns representing five universities.

Post Properties has structured the program to assure it is setting interns up for success by providing a supportive, structured environment. It begins with eight hours online training before interns arrive, then a five-day training program in a classroom. Each intern is assigned a mentor — someone to whom the students can reach out to when they need to better understand how the company operates. Mentors also keep the interns are on track with their tasks, such as interviewing managers, speaking with maintenance people to learn about their job, attending meetings and following through with leasing responsibilities. Interns visit different properties and are given a checklist, so they know exactly what special tasks they need to accomplish during their tenure.

Lori Addicks, vice president in charge of learning and development for Post Properties says, "The idea is to have a framework so students can get assistance when they need it — like a safety net. Having the checklist assists them to accomplish their tasks and help them juggle it all as well."

Feedback is excellent. Students said they were able to hit the ground running because they had a clear purpose, clear expectations and knew where they were headed. The program has consistently exceeded interns' expectations.

"Our hope is to give them a sense of what it's like to work in property management and see if there might be a fit for some of them to return as full-time employees. We have hired a number of interns, and some students even come to work for us on a part-time basis before they finish school," Lori says. "We are investing in both their future and the company's."

REFLECTIONS
CHAPTER TEN

HIGHLIGHTS
CHAPTER TEN

CREATE A ROTATIONAL INTERNSHIP PROGRAM

Rotational internships programs allow young
professionals an opportunity to explore their interests
and gain experience across your organization.

Interns have the opportunity to gain skills and experience
while building a reputation for themselves.

Interships allow the organization and its seasoned professionals
the opportunity to "test drive" young professionals and determine
what position, if any, will best suit their talents.

Here are some important tips for
creating rotational internship programs:

Tip One: Provide Opportunities Early and Often

Tip Two: Create Community Among Interns —
When we feel connected and a part of a team,
we're more likely to want to stay engaged.

Tip Three: Provide a Mentor

Tip Four: Request Feedback —
What's Working/What's Not

Tip Five: Use a Minimum of Four Rotations —
Two years — Provide Options

Tip Six: Create a Well-Structured Process

**Tip Seven: Finding Interns is Easy —
With the Right Process**

Rotational internships programs allow young
professionals an opportunity to explore their interests
and gain experience across your organization.

The organization and seasoned professionals have the
opportunity to "test drive" young professionals and determine
what position, if any, will best suit their talents.

11

THE WIN-WIN OF
MENTORSHIP PROGRAMS

The vast majority of today's young professionals, particularly those just out of school, have enjoyed a network naturally provided to them during every step of their journey. Educational systems encourage interaction among students, and between students and teachers. Students usually have an advisor to help them choose a major and select appropriate classes, and many classes require group work. If students don't want to or don't know how to initiate or build relationships, there's still a good chance they will meet people simply by going to class or living in the dormitory.

Then with no real understanding of how companies function, no clear career goals and a lack of people skills, these young adults enter the workforce. They've been told they can be, do and have anything they want but they were never shown the process by which to do so. When they wanted something, it was simply handed to them. They have been guided and rewarded just for being on the team. Suddenly that support system is gone. Now they're expected to immediately understand how to navigate a new organizational culture, unassisted. When they don't do so "properly," they're considered annoying and "unwilling to pay their dues."

Combine this lack of support with a minimal understanding of corporate culture and you have a generational clash.

Whether young workers' need for guidance and support is "right" or "wrong" is irrelevant. Likewise, seasoned professionals' lack of understanding of technology is neither "right" nor "wrong." Both sides simply require support in different areas. The good news is that they can help one another. Seasoned professionals offer invaluable experience, excellent people skills and big picture perspective. Young professionals possess incredible technology skills, energy, enthusiasm and a fresh perspective.

When we take the focus off "right" vs. "wrong" and put it on what's truly important — the vision/mission of the organization and the individuals working for it — we see **there is a tremendous opportunity to leverage the strengths of every generation.**

Organizations that create opportunities for professionals to understand and relate to each other, and allow for the strengths of each generation to flourish, will meet with success beyond comprehension. Move the focus away from, "We don't get it," **to "Here is how *we* can do it."**

I've often heard seasoned professionals say, "Young professionals focus on themselves and couldn't care less about the company." While young professionals certainly have a long way to go in how they request training and advancement, when they do receive it, both the organization and the employee benefit. As individuals grow and learn, the company increases its abilities to serve customers better and faster.

> *"Mentoring is a brain to pick, an ear to listen, and a push in the right direction."*
>
> JOHN C. CROSBY

When organizations put the right structures in place, such as mentoring programs, to meet the needs of today's young professionals, they will be create an enthusiastic, hard-working, loyal and dedicated group of new employees. Instead of lamenting, "This is the way it has always been done," ask, **"How can we create an environment in which every person can reach his or her potential?"** Remember: When *individuals* in organizations reach *their* goals, the organization also reaches *its* goals. It is a win/win situation.

A program in which seasoned professionals can *opt into* mentoring young professionals gives seasoned professionals an opportunity to share their knowledge, experience, expertise and ideas. It allows young professionals to receive valuable input from their mentors, share their own energy and enthusiasm and get the overall guidance they want and need.

Seasoned mentors can provide a safe environment where young professionals can obtain important feedback and learn how to best navigate the cultural system. A mentor's role is to provide perspective, rather than dictate orders. Every organization has its own process for getting things done. Seasoned professionals understand this and can help guide young professionals.

One of the most important things I encourage young professionals to learn is that it's not *what* you say, it's *how* you say it; it's not *what* you ask for, it's *how* you ask for it. For example, many young professionals request training and development courses, want to attend high profile meetings and want to work within their own timeframes. Many enter their supervisor's office requesting these experiences by saying, "I want this or that training," or "I want to attend a particular meeting," or "I want to work from home."

Mentors can teach their mentees not only what to ask for but *how* to make the request. They help the mentee align personal goals with corporate goals. Imagine a young staffer came into your office saying, "I've been thinking about the long-term goals for the company. In order to help our customers best meet their needs, it might be helpful for our organization to have someone skilled in this particular area; may I take this training?"

In the latter example, the employee asking for training comes across as a team players rather than a selfish brat. **A seasoned mentor can help young professionals gain important perspective in a non-threatening way.**

Over the years, I have come across many organizations that have been unable to successfully implement a mentoring program. After about 10 minutes of discussion, I can usually determine where they could add some additional features that would make such an effort a huge success. Without going into depth, here are some important tips for creating successful mentorship programs:

TIP ONE: ENGAGE LEADERSHIP

Leaders set the stage for every initiative. When leaders are engaged, others see the effort as important and worth getting involved in. Likewise, if leadership is unwilling to participate, the program is less likely to succeed. Leaders can talk about the importance of succession planning and developing the next generation all they want. When they actually choose to participate as mentors, their actions speak much louder than any words. When leaders are involved, others want to get involved, too.

Thomas J. Delong, et. al. emphasize the need for young professionals to find a mentor, in the *Harvard Business Review* article, "Why Mentoring Matters in a Hypercompetitive World" (January 2008). "In today's professional service firms, associates can no longer just expect to be assigned a mentor; they also have to learn how to attract one."

If you are having difficulty finding mentors to participate, engage your leaders and help them understand the importance of their involvement. Also, as with any program, both mentors and mentees need to see what's in it for them. Create a simple marketing plan to help them see what they will get from participating and **share success stories.** People are inspired by others' experiences and are more likely to get involved. Of course, engaging leadership to help you get the message out will help tremendously.

TIP TWO: MENTORS MUST BE *OPT IN* ONLY

Not everyone wants to be a mentor — nor is everyone suited to the part. If an employee doesn't want to be a mentor, don't force it. Clearly explain the process involved in mentoring and let participants know support is available. Demonstrate the personal reward in participating in such a program. **The right people will get involved** (those who want to mentor) and will do a great job.

As people begin talking about how great it is to mentor, your organization will likely see an increased interest in participation. Many people need to see evidence of a support structure before they will get involved. Fortunately, your mentoring program will be around for years to come and they can participate when they are ready.

TIP THREE: TRAINING FOR MENTORS

Mentors must get training on how to be a mentor and how to receive reverse (cross generational) mentoring, regardless of experience.

Many times people who volunteer to mentor have no real understanding of how to do so successfully. Some think mentoring is simply about giving advice and don't understand how to handle certain situations, regardless of experience level or age. Set the stage for success; **provide mentors with a strong training workshop.**

TIP FOUR: SUPPORT FOR MENTORS

Many times, mentors come across situations with their mentee that they don't know how to address. **Having a professional coach available to mentors for support** is enormously beneficial and helps mentors feel they are supported in the mentoring process.

TIP FIVE: TRAINING FOR MENTEES

Mentees must get training on how to be mentored and how to offer reverse (cross generational) mentoring.

As with their mentors, mentees can make assumptions about what it means to participate in a mentoring program and what they can expect. Some mentees might think their mentor is supposed to help them get a promotion or tell them exactly what to do. Many will not even know what questions to ask or how to ask them. **Provide mentees with training on how to get the most out of the relationship with their mentor.**

As in any good relationship, there are always opportunities for both parties to learn from one another. As I mentioned above, young professionals have skills and ideas to share with seasoned professionals. Knowing the best way to communicate those ideas in order to *create opportunities* for shared learning is important. If there is no chance for shared learning, neither side will think it's appropriate and, therefore, never take advantage of this opportunity.

TIP SIX: CREATE A SOLID AND SPECIFIC PROGRAM

People who understand what to expect are more likely to get involved. Simply saying "sign up to be a mentor," without explaining what it means to be a mentor, creates confusion and employees are less apt to get involved. Explain **exactly what both the mentor and mentee can expect so they know what they're opting into.** To get started, I recommend a program like the following:

- *Mentors and mentees can expect to meet as a group four times per year on ____ dates for ____ time. Two of these meetings are half day trainings (how to be a mentor/how to be a mentee)*

- *Mentors and mentees are expected to meet for one-hour every month for one year*

- *Topics to cover in one-on-one mentoring sessions include: career planning; challenges that mentees may be encountering; individuals who may be useful business connections; strategies for gaining exposure/experience.*

- *The mentor program will end on X date with a final award/recognition program.*

(You can view an example of a mentor program at *www.inspirioninc. com/mentorprograms.*)

TIP SEVEN: APPROPRIATE PAIRING

While direct supervisors can provide guidance and certainly some mentoring, **it's important that the mentor for this program *not* be the mentee's direct supervisor. The mentor should be in a higher position than the mentee and, when possible, in a different chain of command.**

The mentor must be able to offer ideas/suggestions, make introductions and provide support for the mentee. There's a great deal more freedom to share frustrations and gain important feedback when the mentor is not in a direct management position.

If the mentee has clear aspirations of moving up inside their current division, it might make sense to provide a mentor who is currently in a high-ranking position in that division or someone who has previously held that position.

TIP EIGHT: HAVE FUN

Mentor/mentee relationships can extend beyond work/career conversations. You might consider planning other relationship building activities such as lunch, golf, shopping or whatever fits well with both of your interests. The intention is to **create an atmosphere where the mentors and mentees can deepen their relationship outside the framework of career and the workplace.** People help people they like; an ideal way to build strong bonds between people is to allow them to get to know each other in a fun way.

WE NEVER GOT MENTORED

I have heard several seasoned professionals say, "We had to figure it out on our own. We didn't get mentoring; why should we mentor them?"

While I can imagine every generation wants(ed) mentoring, today's young professionals need it more than ever. Recent Census data states that **for every two Baby Boomers leaving the workforce only one young professional will fill their spot, thereby creating a great need for knowledge transfer.**

> "The meeting of two personalities is like the contact of two chemical substances: if there is any reaction, both are transformed."
>
> CARL JUNG

In fact, a 2005 Hewitt Associates study entitled "Next-Generation Talent Management" determined that by the year 2010 (only two years away from publication of this volume), there will be 10 million more jobs than workers in the United States alone. As a result, the competition to attract and retain talent is becoming a major focal point for many organizations.

When you focus on your organization/team's long-term success, you see the importance of mentoring young professionals.

Tony Wolfe, an executive with a major financial institution says, "Why would you want to perpetuate a negative cycle? If you didn't receive mentoring, break the cycle and leave a positive legacy. Treat your young professionals the way you wanted to be treated when you entered the workforce."

> *"Create the kind of climate in your organization where personal growth is expected, recognized and rewarded."*
>
> AUTHOR UNKNOWN

Is it possible that you could get something out of being a mentor? Absolutely!

One by-product of mentoring is the satisfaction of helping someone learn, watching them succeed and helping the company develop and retain talent. In turn, the mentee has the opportunity to share their knowledge and information, particularly in the field of new technologies, and infuse the relationship with a refreshing dose of vigor and enthusiasm.

REFLECTIONS
CHAPTER ELEVEN

HIGHLIGHTS
CHAPTER ELEVEN

THE WIN-WIN OF MENTORSHIP PROGRAMS

There is tremendous opportunity to leverage
the strengths of every generation.

As individuals grow and learn, the company increases
its abilities to serve the customer better and faster.

Providing a program in which seasoned professionals
can opt into mentoring young professionals does two things:
- Gives seasoned professionals an opportunity
  to share their knowledge, experience, expertise
  and ideas.
- Provides young professionals the guidance
  they need and want, and allows them to share
  their energy and enthusiasm.

A seasoned mentor can help young professionals gain
important perspective in a non-threatening way.

Here are some important tips for creating mentorship programs:

Tip One: Engage Leadership.

Tip Two: Mentors must be opt in only.

Tip Three: Provide Training for Mentors.

Tip Four: Have a professional coach available to mentors for support.

Tip Five: Training for Mentees.

Tip Six: Create a Solid and Specific Program.

Tip Seven: Appropriate Pairing.

Tip Eight: Have Fun!

For every two Baby Boomers leaving the workforce only one young professional will fill their spot.

When you focus on your organization/team's long-term success, you will see the importance of mentoring young professionals.

PROMOTING AND RECEIVING CROSS-GENERATIONAL MENTORING

I will never forget what it was like leaving college and entering the workforce. In my naive worldview, seasoned professionals were *supposed* to help me. I assumed, first, that they *wanted* to help me and, second, that I had nothing to offer them.

Eventually, I began to see that **everyone — regardless of age or experience — needs assistance in some area.** More important, regardless of your age or experience level, you probably have something valuable to offer almost anyone. Sharing that wisdom can make all the difference in the world for someone who needs it.

Requiring assistance isn't a bad thing. We simply can't know how to do everything!

When a young professional mentors an older professional, we often refer to it as "reverse mentoring." What's interesting, however, is that good mentoring uses the same principles no matter who is mentoring whom. Therefore, it's more appropriate to talk about **cross-generational mentoring," which occurs when people of different generations are mentoring each other.**

I have observed that both younger *and* seasoned professionals essentially are saying, "Meet me where I am, instead of where you think I 'should' be. Assume I mean well (I'm doing the best *I* can) and be patient with me as I learn."

Seasoned professionals are impatient with young professionals who don't understand how the professional world really works — i.e., that it's not likely you will get the corner office in six months, that you have to show credibility over time, etc. On the other hand, young professionals forget that seasoned professionals didn't grow up with technology and become impatient with their lack of skills. Misunderstanding leads to making poor assumptions, which, in turn, affects how people communicate.

If you're interested in establishing a cross-generational mentoring relationship, help your professionals understand its value. It's important to set the stage appropriately, creating a groundwork of understanding and **ensuring that both sides are aware of the strengths they bring to the table.** Young professionals who assume a seasoned professional doesn't want their help need to be shown the opposite is true. Be clear about goals and expectations and remember that recognizing the different communication styles can sometimes be the biggest challenge of all.

> *"If you would thoroughly know anything, teach it to others."*
>
> TRYON EDWARDS

After sending out a monthly newsletter on bridging the generational gap, one of my seasoned readers, Gina, asked me to help her young professionals learn how to mentor seasoned professionals without offending them. She was in the midst of taking a computer training program taught by young professionals and was frustrated with their impatience. While she found their communication style disrespectful, she really wanted to learn from them.

In December 2007, *HR News* quoted Leadership IQ Chairman and

CEO Mark Murphy, "Mangers cannot use one management style and expect success, because every age group is motivated very differently." (Kathy Gurchick, "Praise Goes Far to Motivate Gen Y")

If you're in a mentoring relationship with someone of a **different generation, recognize they grew up in a different world and, as a result, see the world differently.** If they act or react in "inappropriate" ways, don't take it personally.

Seasoned professionals being mentored by younger professionals should simply let them know that while you really *want* to understand, you don't and you need them to slow down.

Young professionals being mentored by seasoned professionals may find it helpful to articulate your needs and expectations, as they may be different than what your mentor has in mind.

> "The competencies of both generations are valuable tools in the marketplace."
>
> SANDRA ALLEN O'CONNOR
> *VP/GM Boston office of Personnel International Corporation*

If your mentor says something that offends you, do as Don Miguel Ruiz suggests in *The Four Agreements* and don't take it personally. Help your mentor understand by explaining what comments come across negatively to you. Ask them what they meant by their statement. It may be that what they meant and what you understood were two different things. Remember, people mean well, but have a different understanding and perspective. The only way they will appreciate your perspective is for you to share it with them.

Here's a simple way to transform your mentoring conversations:

· *Even if you are convinced otherwise, realize that the person means well; they just don't understand how they are coming across.*

· *Shift from reacting to responding. Get curious and ask questions; don't take comments personally).*

· *Without feedback, no one will ever know you are upset. Let it be known you recognize that what was said was well intended, and share how it came across to you.*

- *Help them see a new way to communicate with you that is effective. If you simply say, "You're not communicating well," they won't know what to do differently.*

- *Young professionals often need to slow down so they don't overwhelm those whom they are mentoring.*

- *Continue learning and growing together, knowing that you have much to offer each other.*

When people of different generations communicate effectively with the goal of understanding each other's viewpoints, they are able to move toward their common vision and have successful and rewarding interactions, not only in a mentoring relationship, but also in daily exchanges.

~ AN AWARD-WINNING CROSS-GENERATIONAL MENTORSHIP PROGRAM AND PROMOTING A CULTURE SHIFT ~

This is an optimistic story of a huge government contractor/technology company that was heavily imbued with "old school" politics and the military style of "command and control."Like most companies, the majority of its senior professionals would be retiring over the next 10 years. In order to survive, it must learn how to recruit, retain and work with the "new breed" of young professionals joining the workforce.

To get the ball rolling, in 2006 its forward thinking CIO established a set of goals: "Expand IT mentoring of diversity employees and include reverse mentoring to enhance multi-generational inclusion."

Her bold objectives manifested, at first, in a very small way. One courageous seasoned professional, Ted, went to one young professional, Cheryl, and asked to be mentored by her.

At first, they ended each session with Cheryl saying, "Wait a minute … You have been mentoring me all this time and I was supposed to be mentoring you!" And they would agree to try again at their next meeting.

They were truly stepping out of their comfort zones, and company culture, in order to facilitate growth. Because what they were attempting was so "outside the box," they decided to document it for the benefit of their co-workers and the company as a whole. They believed that if they could create a functional system for mentoring across generations, they would be able to help other departments do the same. As a result of their work together, Cheryl's job is now to facilitate a shift in corporate culture.

Engineers — generally not "people focused" individuals — would eventually become managers with no training or preparation. Needless to say, leadership skills were not their strong suit, so they continued to focus primarily on their engineering duties and let the leadership part take care of itself.

As a result, turnover levels among young professionals were high. These individuals couldn't put up with the lack of feedback, direction and interesting assignments. Seasoned professionals saw their young colleagues' enthusiasm for the work, but realized they would be responsible for any mistakes the young workers might make. The seasoned workers were the first ones to arrive in the morning and the last ones to leave. It was easier for them to do the work themselves than to spend hours they didn't have reworking someone else's mistakes.

"It's a perfect storm," Cheryl says. "Young people have incredible skills that most Boomers do not have. And Boomers have communication skills, a bird's eye view of the company and have already built relationships. Contrary to what many young professionals believe, the seasoned professionals are not slow or inefficient. They continue to put in a lot of hours, they are always the 'last ones standing.'"

At present, Cheryl explains, the company is only hiring a "half person" to cover each person leaving. That means one college graduate with no experience is doing the work of two experienced senior people. "It is critical for young professionals to ask about the process, the lessons to be learned and learn the mind-set around why the seasoned professionals do things the way they do," Cheryl says.

To help with this shift, engineers in management are being refocused. They now spend the majority of their time on managing a team rather than working on projects themselves. They are learning to manage a team structure and being forced to teach and mentor. Wisely, the entire leadership team has been assigned external coaches to ensure the effort's success.

Cheryl coaches senior professionals to talk with a young professional several times each week. She and Ted put together some ice breaking questions to get things started:

- *How are you motivated at work?*

- *What de-motivates you?*

- *How do you like to be rewarded?*

- *What are the first things you consider when making an important decision at work?*

- *How do you determine who you can trust at work?*

- *What changes do you think we could make at our organization that would improve employee retention?*

- *What are your thoughts about loyalty to the company?*

- *What's more important to you, salary or title? Why?*

- *How do you feel about using technology to communicate? When to, when not to?*

Once the parties get to know each other, they employ these "weekly challenges" to continue the exploration and relationship building process:

- *(Gen Y) Ask the Boomer about something they experienced with a Gen Y that you might be able to provide some advice or insight on.*

- *(Boomer) Share an experience you had with a Gen Y that didn't turn out the way you had expected or that you think could have gone better.*

- *(Gen Y) Discuss how you would have handled it differently. Provide alternate approaches and a Gen Y perspective of the scenario.*

- *(Together) Determine how you will create opportunities between now and your next meeting to practice this newly suggested approach.*

- *Begin the next meeting with a follow up of the above discussion. Did the Boomer apply the new approach? What was the result?*

- *Repeat this pattern as long as desired.*

Cheryl's job is to help the team build relationships and bridge gaps. When someone comes to her disgruntled about a situation, her favorite question to ask is, "What can we do right now to turn this around?" She turns the responsibility toward the individual and gets them thinking creatively about solutions.

REFLECTIONS

CHAPTER TWELVE

HIGHLIGHTS
CHAPTER TWELVE

"Cross-Generational Mentoring," occurs when people
of different generations are mentoring each other.

Everyone, regardless of age or experience,
needs assistance in some area.

Regardless of your age or experience level, you probably
have something valuable to offer almost anyone.

People have different experience and different
expertise, and sharing that wisdom can make all the
difference in the world for someone who needs it.

Good mentoring employs the same principles,
no matter who is mentoring whom.

PERSONAL SUCCESS
FOR SEASONED PROFESSIONALS

With so much buzz around generational diversity and retaining young talent, many companies are focusing on young professionals and forgetting about development at *all* levels. I've heard many seasoned professionals express frustration with the constant focus on younger generations, saying that it leaves them unwilling to be as helpful as they could be. An organization that focuses solely on the development of young professionals creates a dichotomy which does a disservice to the organization as a whole.

If organizations want seasoned professionals to engage in developing young professionals, it must show how they, too, will benefit. The best way to create new positions and offer opportunities to young professionals is to keep seasoned professionals advancing. **Focusing on the development of all employees demonstrates a commitment to everyone.** Supporting professionals on both sides of the generational bridge is important for creating camaraderie and teamwork.

This point was demonstrated during a discussion I had with 150 human resources professionals on how to retain young talent. Janet, a Generation Xer, stood up and said, "I do not want to share my knowledge or develop the skills of younger professionals in my organization. If I share my knowledge and expertise with them, they will take my job." Janet was likely not the only person in the room who felt that way; she was simply the only one willing to say it out loud.

After acknowledging her for the courage to stand up and share, I asked if she would be willing to be coached in front of the group. To my surprise, she said, "Yes." With her agreement, I began asking her a series of questions, "Do you care about the success of your organization?" She quickly responded with "Yes." I said, "OK, great! Do you understand the importance of knowledge transfer for the long-term success of the company?" Again, she responded with, "Yes, but I don't want to teach them what I know because then they'll take my job."

I went on to ask her, "What is your five-year-plan?" Her face dropped a bit and she looked puzzled. I continued with, "Do you have career goals for five years from now?" Her response, "No." I asked, "Do you have a six-month plan?" She responded with, "To get through the next six months."

I looked at her and said, "How can you get excited about developing those coming up after you, if you have no plan for *your* future?" As Janet nodded in agreement, I suggested that she create a three- to-five-year plan and begin considering where she would like to take her career.

You can begin creating your own plan by simply listing the skills and experiences you would like to gain.

As Janet begins planning for her own future (i.e. what position she would like to be in, what skills she would like to develop and what experiences she would like to gain), she will be much more willing to support, develop, coach and mentor those coming up behind her.

Helping your organization reach its potential requires taking a good look at your own objectives. Before you can effectively and authentically help others develop, you must first look at your career goals and future aspirations. It doesn't matter where you are in your career, **generating a plan for where you want to go will provide you with focus and guidance.** With no plan or strategy for your own success, helping others with their development can feel threatening.

Very few people take the time to think about what they want, why they want it and do the research necessary to understand what "it" *really* is. This process takes time, patience and persistence, and it's well worth it.

I've heard many seasoned professionals say things like, "I've been around long enough, shouldn't I know what I want, where I'm going and why I want it? Doesn't it make me look bad to not know, especially at this stage? Where do I start?" It doesn't matter where you are in your career or stage of life. What does matter is your commitment and courage to begin looking and asking.

When you know where you want to go in your own career and have set some long-term goals for yourself, helping others learn and advance is fun and rewarding — after all, you're moving up, too!

When today's seasoned professionals were just entering the workforce, the number of career options were small in comparison to what's available now. During this time, specific careers were designated for women and going outside the norm was neither accepted nor rewarded. It was expected that you would take the position you were given, work hard, put in your time and, eventually, you might get promoted.

Now those same professionals have been in the workforce for a while, have gained valuable experience and are ready to explore what's next. Because many have never considered what they want, they find themselves stuck taking whatever position(s) come to them without first considering if the job fits their interests.

> "Fall in love with what you are going to do for a living. To be able to get out of bed and do what you love to do for the rest of the day is beyond words. I'd rather be a failure at something I love than be successful in something I hate."
> GEORGE BURNS

This may be true for you, as it is with many of my coaching clients who are seasoned professionals. In fact, if they were given the option to design the "perfect" position, many would have no idea where to begin. **Here are some action steps to help you create a career plan for your future:**

SKILLS

When I first began coaching Sharon, a 45-year-old corporate executive who had been with her company for 25 years, she had never considered what skills she most enjoyed using. Sharon had taken an administrative position with a large telecommunications company directly out of high school.

Over the next quarter-century, she graciously took whatever job was assigned to her and consistently performed well. As a result, Sharon worked her way up to an executive level, was well-respected and finally ready to make a strategic career move. While she was bored in her current position and ready for change, Sharon had no idea what position she was interested in pursuing.

When I first asked her what skills she most enjoyed using, she looked at me blankly — this clearly wasn't something she'd spent much time thinking about. Over the next two weeks Sharon generated a list of 10 skills she had enjoyed using throughout her career.

Here is a list of some of the skills Sharon (and others) created:

- *Writing*

- *Budgeting*

- *Managing a project*

- *Leading people*

- *Presenting*

- *Setting strategy*

- *Analyzing data*

- *Researching*

- *Public speaking*

- *Marketing*

- *Sales*

- *Customer Service*

Armed with a clear list of skills she enjoyed using, I asked her to create a list of skills she would like to develop and experiences she would like to gain. Not surprisingly, that was a much easier task.

JOBS

Once Sharon finished the list of skills she most enjoyed using and the skills she wanted to develop, we began thinking about a position that would fit her best. Because she had stayed so narrowly focused on her work, she'd never taken notice of what other positions entailed. As a result, she needed to begin the information-gathering phase, including conducting some informational interviews.

An "informational interview" provides a way to meet individuals who are a field that interests you. This simple technique allows you to speak with a knowledgeable professional about their field, their career and to find out if you might enjoy working in that field yourself.

Though Sharon was unfamiliar with the potential jobs within her company, many people are aware of what positions would fit them best, even if they are unsure how to move into them. For those of you in this situation, the next step is a little more specific and targeted. Your informational interviews will be with those currently in the position you most desire. If that approach doesn't make sense to you (perhaps you don't want the person to become worried you are trying to take their job), interview someone who has held that job before, the supervisor for that position or a person in that position at a *different* company. Remember, your intention is to gather additional information about what the job entails, while, of course, developing relationships along the way.

INFORMATIONAL INTERVIEWS/NETWORKING

Because Sharon was unclear as to what career opportunities were available within her company, I encouraged her to select a few colleagues to speak with in order to gain their perspective. Be sure you prepare your interviewee for your questions by letting him/her know why you are requesting an interview (calling a meeting). If, for example, you **let the person know that you are considering your next career move, but are unsure as to the best position for you,** s/he will be more receptive to your questions.

Below is a list of questions to consider when conducting informational interviews at this stage in your career:

- *Tell me about your career — how did you get to where you are?* This question will provide you with ample opportunity to hear about the many positions the person has held throughout her career. As you listen, you can probe further about what, specifically, she did in those positions.

- *What, specifically, are your current job duties?*

- *What do you most enjoy about your current position?*

- *What do you least enjoy about your current position?*

- *Recently I discovered I most enjoy using _____ skills — what position utilizes these skills most?* You might also let them know about the skills/experiences you would like to gain and request their feedback on the positions that would fit best.

- *Can you think of others who might be good for me to interview?* Sometimes no one comes to mind at the moment, so let them know you will send an email with the specifics about what you are looking for and ask them to think about someone to introduce you to.

- *What experiences/skills do you think I need to gain in order to get into my ideal position? What is the best way to gain those experiences/skills?*

- *With those you trust, consider asking — can I share my long-term goals with you in order to gain your perspective?*

After seven months of informational interviews and searching for a new career direction, Sharon determined that a position which allowed her to connect with customers, experience the sales side of the business and lead a different group people in another type of environment, would suit her future ambitions. She achieved her goals via her new position as sales center vice president, acquired with the assistance of a person with whom she had held an informational interview.

Here's another great story how a little investigation and relationship building goes a long way. Glen, who had been in the same position for more than five years with a *Fortune* 50 company, also used informational interviews as a strategy to move forward on his career path.

Glen wanted to move up in the company and was at a loss for why he wasn't being promoted. He was very smart, clearly personable, willing to work hard and a good team player. At first, I, too, couldn't understand why he was being held back. Finally, I realized that he was not a good self-promoter, had little understanding of what he wanted to do next or long-term and was simply "hoping" to get noticed and promoted.

When I asked Glen where he would like to be in the next five years, he quickly responded with "three levels above where I am currently — a VP." Then, when I asked why, he had no real answer — he didn't know why.

Over several coaching sessions, he began considering his dream career. Due to fear of failure, Glen was reluctant to admit that what he truly loved was the mergers and acquisitions (M&A, or the buying and selling of companies) aspect of running a big company.

As he began talking about the process of buying and selling companies, Glen got very excited. I could clearly see that he loved the idea of looking at a business and deciding whether it would be worth purchasing. His whole face lit up as he talked about all the studying he had done over the past several years while getting his Masters of Business Administration.

While Glen thought it would be a long time before he could actually begin working in M&A, he stayed focused on simply gaining knowledge about the field. Over the next few weeks, I requested that he begin doing research on all the different aspects of M&A. He looked into the banking side, M&A internal to his organization and began using his network to conduct informational interviews to learn more.

Glen used his connections to set up informational interviews both inside and outside his current company. One of the interviews included the

VP of M&A within his company, which was a position that attracted his interest. Although Glen was being offered jobs within less than six weeks, he wasn't yet ready to make a decision — he was still learning about the M&A business. His enthusiasm for learning about mergers and acquisitions carried into the interviews and led other companies to offer him a job, even though he wasn't looking.

Glen later learned about an opportunity in the corporate strategy group, an integral part of his company's M&A process. The exciting part about the new opportunity is that unbeknownst to Glen, two senior executives with whom he had conducted informational interviews recommended him for the new position.

Few people invest in informational interviews. They may be unsure as to how to go about conducting them, don't know who to interview or lack the self-esteem to make the request. However, setting up an interview is easier than you may think — successful individuals enjoy conversations with enthusiastic people *and* most people enjoy talking about themselves. You can obtain valuable information when you are truly there just to listen.

Also, keep in mind that people are most interested in what you can do for them. In the business world, this is referred to as **"What's In It For Me" (or WIIFM).** The reality is, we're all concerned with "what's in it for me," even when we're being generous. If you understand this concept, then you can tell people what they want to hear: the value *you* bring to them or to their organization. If you can **help them attain something they are seeking** (perhaps a skill, or simply a positive, enthusiastic attitude), you can create a relationship that will last well beyond the interview! Informational interviews can be a huge part of your success, as they have been — and continue to be — both for me, and the many people I coach.

As you can see, informational interviews can be a critical component of your career development in many different ways!

GOALS

Once you have gained clarity regarding position(s) that best fit your interests, it's time to **set some long- and short-term goals.** During a coaching session with Tom, an engineer and executive with a *Fortune* 50 company, I asked him to develop a five-year career plan. Two weeks later, Tom, came to our next session with a one-sheet plan for his future. I liked it so much it is available for free at *www.inspirioninc.com/ppt/careermap.ppt*

Essentially, what Tom did was create a visual plan to hit his target. Here are the steps he took:

- *Clearly defined the position level he wanted to achieve and set a target date.*

- *Identified those currently in that level — this was helpful in gaining their perspective regarding what he needed to do to get the promotion he wanted.*

- *Identified those capable of sponsoring/helping him get into that position.*

- *Made note of the skills he needed to gain to be successful in that position.*

- *Made note of the experiences he needed to gain to be successful in that position.*

- *Began targeted networking to share his big goals.*

- *Became active in helping others reach their goals (i.e. mentoring).*

BRAG — BE CLEAR, SPECIFIC AND TARGETED

Many people are afraid to share their long-term goals. If they don't make it, they fear others will know they failed. While it's true that if they never say anything, no one will ever know they missed the mark, it's also true that no one will be there to support them in the process or know when they have succeeded!

Tom took a *huge* step forward and began targeted marketing for his goal. After locating people in a position to help him in reach his career objectives, he began **developing relationships, sharing his current successes**

and his future aspirations, including taking the Human Resources Director to lunch.

Once you're clear about your short and long-term goals, it's time to **talk about your goals with the people who can make a difference.** Of course, it's also important to **ensure they are aware of your current successes.**

Many people are afraid of being perceived as "bragging," having been raised to keep a low profile about their accomplishments. What they fail to realize is that *no one will know* about their accomplishments if they never share. Women, especially, find this difficult. Many assume someone will eventually notice their hard work and great results and bestow upon them a promotion to the exact position they want. They do this is without clearly articulating their idea of the perfect position, or sharing about their successes. As a result, many of these people remain unacknowledged, disappointed and even resentful. Often when they do get promoted, it's to a position that really doesn't excite them. Speak up!

By the way, as a result of Tom's efforts, he's being considered for positions that are in alignment with exactly what he wants.

LOCATE SPONSORS/MENTORS

While most people like the idea of having mentors/sponsors, few understand how to find someone willing to mentor/sponsor them. **The key is to find someone you respect who's in a position to guide you and willing to give you some of their time.** Finding a sponsor requires one additional consideration — the person must be in a position higher than yours and able to help you get promotions and visibility.

Finding a mentor/sponsor is less about asking someone to mentor you and more about finding someone you respect and talking with them about their success (a process similar to an informational interview). Inquire about other successful professionals within your organization and learn more about them. Ask yourself if these are people you respect and want to learn from. As you find people with common values, stay focused on the qualities you most admire. Once you begin looking around for potential mentors/sponsors, you may be amazed how many qualified people you find.

Once you locate these people, ask them to go to coffee/lunch with you and be prepared to ask questions in order to learn more about them. For example, "How did you get to your current position?" "What are some of your 'secrets' to your success?" "What ideas/suggestions can you offer to help me get to…?"

These questions naturally foster a mentoring relationship and once you develop a rapport, you can request another meeting. If the individual can't find time in their schedule immediately, be patient. If they reschedule several times, don't take it personally. Just keep rescheduling and eventually you'll have your meeting.

I remember asking Jane, senior vice president of human resources at a *Fortune* 5 company, to let me take her to lunch. She said, "Sure, speak with my assistant and have her find some time on my schedule." Two months later and one week before my scheduled time with Jane, her assistant called to reschedule — something had come up. This happened three or four times in a row. It would have been easy for me to take it personally and assume she really didn't want to meet with me. Instead, I kept rescheduling and I eventually got an hour with Jane, which ended up being hugely beneficial.

The biggest challenge in beginning a mentoring relationship is getting over the socially imposed idea that only weak people request assistance. The opposite is really true. **Only courageous people are brave enough to acknowledge a need for support and guidance,** though we *all* need these! Recognizing that you can't do it all by yourself and requesting assistance from others is a big step toward becoming a great leader.

The most effective and sought after leaders are the ones who know how to engage others. Asking someone for their ideas, support or guidance does two things: It gives the other person an opportunity to feel good about assisting someone on a path to improvement and **it provides you with the help you need to progress.**

Once you find someone you respect and begin to develop a rapport, **stay persistent in getting to know them** *and* **having them get to know you. Look for ways to support them in their goals** (remember WIIFM), as this will strengthen the relationship. Perhaps you can use your network to help them make needed connections.

As you advance in your career, look around for others you can mentor/sponsor — there's always plenty of opportunity. It's a great way to "give back" and people will appreciate the opportunity to learn from you.

REFLECTIONS
CHAPTER THIRTEEN

HIGHLIGHTS
CHAPTER THIRTEEN

The best way to create new positions and offer opportunities to young professionals is to keep your seasoned professionals advancing.

Supporting professionals on both sides of the generational bridge is important toward creating camaraderie or teamwork.

When you know where you want to go in your own career and have set some long-term goals for yourself, helping others learn and advance is fun and rewarding.

Action steps help you create a career plan. Develop a list of skills, jobs, people to interview, career goals, locate sponsors/mentors and brag.

CHAPTER FOURTEEN

CONCLUSION

Leaders and organizations that realize both the world and their employee base are constantly changing and make strategic adjustments accordingly will thrive, regardless of employee shortages or the economy. The organizations that will be the most successful at attracting and retaining talent are the ones whose leaders embrace change, trust their employees, fully consider their ideas and find ways to create alignment.

The international research and management consulting firm, Accenture, in its 2006 High Performance Workforce Study found that "truly talent-powered organizations are adept at defining talent needs, discovering diverse sources of talent, developing individual and collective talents, and deploying talent in ways that align people with strategic objectives."

Creating an effective and productive work environment, where employees at every level and age can thrive, is an ongoing, lengthy process. It requires constant attention to what is working and what isn't, and a willingness to get uncomfortable enough to consistently try new strategies.

On the contrary, any organization or leader who thinks they "get it" and are no longer asking tough questions of their teams and their customers, will soon find themselves without teams to serve those customers. I encourage you to consider how your organization functions and what *you* can do differently to get the results you desire.

Even more important than focusing on how to best attract, retain and motivate the youngest generation for successful companies is the need to focus on development *across* generations. When seasoned professionals have the opportunities they long for and create a plan for their future, they're much more likely to support those coming up after them. Likewise, helping young professionals understand how they can be successful inside your organization (and with seasoned professionals) will provide them with the tools necessary for their success.

> *"If you always do what you've always done, you'll always get what you've always gotten."*
> ANTHONY ROBBINS

Organizations focusing primarily on what seasoned professionals can do to best "deal with" or "tolerate" the younger generation are doing a disservice to all aspects of their organization, and are missing out on critical engagement across generations. This engagement requires that employees from each level and generation be recognized for the important contributions they are making. That allows employees to take an organization from just surviving, all the way to the top of its game.

> *"The important thing is not being afraid to take a chance. Remember, the greatest failure is to not try."*
> DEBBI FIELDS
> *Founder of Mrs. Fields Cookies*

Rather than waiting for the company to make changes, smaller teams inside large organizations can begin taking the steps outlined in this book and use them *today.*

Create regular opportunities for your team to brainstorm the most effective solutions within your current system. As a leader at any level, you can also begin feeding ideas for process improvement to other leaders within your organization to insure that, over time, positive changes will begin taking place.

If the problem is conflict between professionals of different generations, consider bringing them together and creating a renewed vision/mission. Doing this consistently over time — at a minimum, every six months, maintains alignment and keeps your team moving forward. As employees clearly understand where the team is headed and how they contribute, they will become more productive. Yes, taking team members away from their work to focus on the bigger picture will allow them to be more effective long-term.

Encouraging each employee to outline their career aspirations will help your organization and the individuals that comprise it to gain clarity. Creating alignment requires a clear understanding of where both the *organization and the individual* are headed. This clarity will bring great results, particularly to your bottom line!

Please let me know how I can be of assistance to you or your organization. My commitment is to help organizations, teams and leaders around the world develop leadership capabilities and create partnership between generations.

REFERENCES

Best Practices, LLC. *Research Study*. 2003.

SelectMind. *Research Study*. 2006.

Danielson, Diane K. "The Generation Slap." *Pink Magazine*. August/September 2007.

Danielson, Diane K. "Welcome to the Matrix." *Pink Magazine*. August/September 2006.

Deal, Jennifer. *Retiring the Generation Gap, How Employees Young and Old Can Find Common Ground*. San Francisco: John Wiley & Sons, Inc, 2007.

DeLong, Thomas J., John J. Gabarro, and Robert J. Lees. "Why Mentoring Matters in a Hypercompetitive World." *Harvard Business Review*. January 2008.

Einhorn, Bruce. "The Future of Work Managing the New Workforce." *Business Week*. August 20 & 27, 2007.

Friedman, Laurie. "Are You Losing Potential New Hires at Hello?" *T+D*. November 2006.

American Institutes for Research. *Research Study*. (date unknown)

Givray, Henry S. "When CEO's Aren't Leaders." *Business Week*. September 3, 2007.
Gurchick, Kathy. "Praise Goes Far To Motivate Gen Y." *HR News*. December 2007.

Hewitt Associates. *Next-Generation Talent Management.* 2005

Logan, Rebecca. "Making Partner Can Be a Trade-Off for Lawyers." *Washington Business Journal.* June 8-14, 2007.

McLean, Cari. "Generation Y Skill Gaps: The Impact on Performance." *Mediatec Publishing.* March 14, 2006.

Myers, Jennifer. "The How and the Y." *Profit Guide.* October 2007.

O'Connor, Sandra Allen. "Preparing Generation X for Baby Boom Retirements." *Boston Business Journal.* November 9, 2007.

Ruiz, Don Miguel. *The Four Agreements.* San Rafael: Amber-Allen Publishing, 2001.

Smith, W. Stanton. *Decoding Generational Differences: Fact, fiction ... or should we just get back to work?* New York: Deloitte & Touche USA LLP, 2008.

Tulgen, Bruce *The Under-Management Epidemic.* RainmakerThinking, 2004.

Welch, Jack and Suzy. "Which Job is the Right Job?" *Business Week.* May 28, 2007.

Welch, Jack and Suzy. "The importance of Being There." *Business Week.* April 16, 2007.

Gallup statistics. 2004.

SUGGESTED READINGS

INTER-GENERATIONAL MASTERY
Decoding Generational Differences by W. Stanton Smith
Generations at Work by Zemke
Getting Them To Give a Damn by Eric Chester
Managing the Generation Mix by Carolyn Martin
The New Workforce by Harriet Hankin
The Next Revolution by Shelton
Retiring the Generation Gap by Jennifer Deal
Millennial Leaders: Success Stories from Today's Most
    Brilliant Generation Y Leaders (Bea Fields, Scott Wilder,
    Jim Bunch and Rob Newbold [NY: Morgan James, 2008]).

CAREER, BUSINESS AND LEADERSHIP MASTERY
Before You Quit Your Job by Robert Kiyosaki
E-Myth Revisited by Michael Gerber
Exploring Leadership by Susan R. Komives
First Break all the Rules by Marcus Buckingham
How To Win Friends and Influence People by Dale Carnegie
Influence by Robert Cialdini
Leadership From the Inside Out by Cashman
The Long Tail by Chris Anderson
Masters of Success by Ivan R. Misner
Principle Centered Leadership by Stephan Covey
The Quick and Easy Way to Effective Speaking by Dale Carnegie
Thinking for a Change by John Maxwell
The 21 Indispensable Qualities of a Leader by John Maxwell
What Color is your Parachute? by Richard Bolles
What Should I do with My Life? by Po Bronson
Who Are You Really, And What Do You Want? By Shad Helmstetter, PhD.

Winning by Jack and Suzy Welch
Winning With People by John Maxwell
The World is Flat by Thomas Friedman

PERSONAL MASTERY

The Accidental Millionaire by Stephanie Frank
The Art of Possibility by Benjamin Zander
Blink by Malcolm Gladwell
Difficult Conversations by Stone, Patton, Heen
Easier Than You Think by Richard Carlson
Eat. Pray. Love by Elizabeth Gilbert
Face Your Fear by Rabbi Shmuley Boteach
The Four Agreements by Don Miguel Ruiz
Good To Great by Jim Collins
Learned Optimism by Martin E. Seligman
The New Psycho-Cybernetics by Maxwell Maltz
Our Separate Ways by Ella L.J. Edmondson Bell
The Power of Focus by Jack Canfield
The Purpose of your Life by Carol Adrien
She Wins, You Win by Gail Evans
Success Through A Positive Mental Attitude by Napoleon Hill
The Tipping Point by Malcolm Gladwell
Tripping The Prom Queen by Susan Shapiro-Brash
Unlimited Power by Anthony Robbins
You Can Feel Good Again by Richard Carlson

NETWORKING RESOURCES

ASWA — American Society for Women Accountants
http://aswa.org
ASWA National Headquarters
8405 Greensboro Drive, Suite 800
McLean, VA 22102
800/326-2163
703/506-3265
Fax: 703/506-3266

Black Business Professionals and Entrepreneurs
http://www.blackbusinessprofessionals.com/
PO Box 60561
Savannah, Georgia 31420
PH: 912-354-7400

Business Networking International — BNI
www.bni.com
545 College Commerce Way
Upland, CA 91786
PH: 1-800-825-8286
FAX: 1-909-608-7676

Chamber of Commerce
(find your local Chamber)
www.uschamber.com

Collegiate Entrepreneurs Organization
www.c-e-o.org
601 South Morgan Street Suite 709(MC 244)
Chicago, IL 60607-7107
PH: 312-996-2670

eWomen Network
www.ewomennetwork.com
14900 Landmark Boulevard Suite 540
Dallas TX 75254
PH: 972-620-9995

International Young Professionals Foundation
www.iypf.org/index.php
Email Inquiries — iypf@iypf.org
Membership — membership@iypf.org
Human Resources — brittjacobsen@iypf.org
PO Box 4338,
MANUKA ACT 2603, Australia

NAFE (National Association for Female Executives)
www.nafe.com
Customer Service 800-927-6233
Main Office 212-351-6451

NAWBO (National Association for Women Business Owners)
www.nawbo.org
8405 Greensboro Drive Suite #800
McLean VA
800-55-NAWBO

Professional Women of Color Network
www.pwocn.org
PO BOX 22367
Seattle, WA 98122
PH: 206-568-3044 EXT 1

Toastmasters International
www.toastmasters.org/

WIT (Women in Technology)
http://womenintechnology.org
717 Princess Street
Alexandria, VA 22314
PH 703-683-4003

Directory of organizations for young professionals
http://www.ypcommons.org/index.cfm/fuseaction/directory.main

ONLINE NETWORKING GROUPS

www.**networking**for**professionals**.com/
www.Spoke.com
www.Linkedin.com
www.Ryze.com
www.Meetup.com
www.Myspace.com
www.Orkut.com
www.Sermo.com (for physicians)

PHOTOGRAPH BY DARREN LIVINGSTON

Misti L. Burmeister is the CEO and Founder of Inspirion Inc., a company formed to assist organizations on creating systems that attract and retain talent among generations.

Best known as an executive coach and generational diversity consultant, Misti focuses on coaching successful senior leaders in large organizations through leadership transitions. She brings more than a decade of professional experience to her work with executives in companies and organizations.

Misti facilitates leadership development programs, generational diversity and mission development sessions and team-building activities. She conducts workshops and seminars on topics such as strategic networking, career development, powerful communication, self-promotion, mentoring, intergenerational communication and values-based leadership.

Misti is known for her combination of executive leadership experience, business savvy and attentive listening style.

She holds a master's degree and two bachelor's degrees from the University of Northern Colorado.

NOTES

NOTES